A WELL-BUILT FAITH

JOE PAPROCKI

A WELL-BUILT FAITH

A Catholic's Guide to Knowing and Sharing What We Believe

LoyolaPress.
A Jesuit Ministry
Chicago

LOYOLA PRESS.
A JESUIT MINISTRY
3441 N. ASHLAND AVENUE
CHICAGO, ILLINOIS 60657
(800) 621-1008
www.loyolapress.com

Nihil Obstat
Reverend John G. Lodge, SSL, STD
Censor Deputatus
May 9, 2008

Imprimatur
Reverend John F. Canary, STL, DMin
Vicar General
Archdiocese of Chicago
May 12, 2008

The *Nihil Obstat* and *Imprimatur* are official declarations that a book is free of doctrinal and moral error. No implication is contained therein that those who have granted the *Nihil Obstat* and *Imprimatur* agree with the content, opinions, or statements expressed. Nor do they assume any legal responsibility associated with publication.

Cover design by Mia Basile
Interior design by Maggie Hong and Donna Antkowiak

Library of Congress Cataloging-in-Publication Data
Paprocki, Joe.
A well-built faith: a Catholic's guide to knowing and sharing what we believe / Joe Paprocki.
p. cm.
ISBN-13: 978-0-8294-2757-8
ISBN-10: 0-8294-2757-0
1. Catholic Church—Doctrines. 2. Theology, Doctrinal—Popular works. I. Title.
BX1754.P34 2008
282—dc22

2008014205

Printed in USA
08 09 10 11 12 13 RRD 10 9 8 7 6 5 4 3 2 1

Dedication

I dedicate this book to my brothers and sisters:

Ramona, Jim, Tom, Ed, John, Ron, Al, and Ann.

As kids, we built many things together, but none as enduring

as the faith that is built by a loving family.

Thanks for building me up.

Contents

PART THREE—THE MORAL LIFE: LIVING FAITH

PART FOUR—PRAYER: PRAYING FAITH

Acknowledgments

I would like to thank Joe Durepos for tenaciously pursuing the right formula for this book and to all of the folks at Loyola Press for helping to build it. Many thanks to Doug Hall for his wonderful cartoons, which capture the lighter moments of church life. Special thanks to the people most responsible for building my faith over the years: my Mom and Dad; the Sisters of the Resurrection and the lay teachers of Saint Casimir grade school; the Jesuits and lay teachers of Saint Ignatius College Prep and Loyola University of Chicago; the faculty of the Institute of Pastoral Studies at Loyola University of Chicago, the Catholic Theological Union at Chicago, and the University of Saint Mary of the Lake, Mundelein Seminary; my wife Jo; and the Holy Spirit.

Introduction—A Little H.E.L.P.

The Right Tools and a Firm Foundation

I was getting my tires changed on my car one day and, as I sat in the waiting room at the auto mechanic, I noticed something interesting. There before me was an entire wall filled with framed certificates for all of the mechanics on duty. It seems that they had been trained in the knowledge and skills needed to service cars properly. They had not only learned how to use the right tools as mechanics, but they had also, through their training, acquired a firm foundation for getting the job done properly. What was even more impressive was that some of the mechanics who had been working there for some time had continued to compile certificates. As technology and cars progressed and changed, so too did the mechanics.

We Catholics seek to be people who have the right tools and a firm foundation to serve God and others. How do we do this? Through faith formation. Catechesis is the process through which we become equipped with the right tools and a firm foundation to live out our baptism. This is a process that is never finished—it is ongoing and lifelong. We all need to start somewhere. That's where *A Well-Built Faith: A Catholic's Guide to Knowing and Sharing What We Believe* comes in. This book is designed to give you a firm foundation to get started in a lifelong process of developing a well-built faith. Whether you are a catechist, a liturgical minister, a parish pastoral council member, a catechumen or candidate in the RCIA, or an everyday Catholic trying to remain faithful to your baptismal call and grow closer to the Lord, *A Well-Built Faith* is designed for you, "so that the one who belongs to God may be competent, equipped for every good work" (2 Timothy 3:17).

A firm foundation provides support for that which is built upon it. In ancient times, pillars provided the support for mammoth structures that would otherwise collapse under the weight of tons of building materials. When it comes to our faith, the Catholic Church has arranged a vast array of doctrines and beliefs into a somewhat mammoth structure we know as the *Catechism of the Catholic Church*. This structure is supported by four pillars, which provide a firm foundation for our faith.

1. **The Creed**
2. **The Sacraments**
3. **The Moral Life**
4. **A Life of Prayer**

This simple organization of over 2000 years of a living Tradition provides us with easy access to our faith. At the same time, the *Catechism of the Catholic Church*, at over 900 pages long, was not written with the average Catholic as its targeted reader. Rather, it was written as a reference book for bishops and for those who teach the Catholic faith. With that in mind, the bishops of the United States produced a more readable resource, the *United States Catholic Catechism for Adults* (2006), which follows the organization of the *Catechism of the Catholic Church*. Even so, the *United States Catholic Catechism for Adults* weighs in at over 600 pages, still a daunting task for many readers. Catholics continue to ask for help in learning about their faith in a way that makes it accessible. With this book, *A Well-Built Faith*, help has arrived.

The *Catechism of the Catholic Church* is arranged in four parts: "The Profession of Faith"; "The Celebration of the Christian Mystery"; "Life in Christ"; and "Christian Prayer."

(*USCC for Adults, pg. xvii*)

A Little H.E.L.P.

Shortly after the events of September 11, 2001, there was a great deal of tension between Muslims and non-Muslims in many parts of the United States. In an effort to respond to the situation with Gospel values, I invited the Imam of a local Muslim community in the Chicago suburbs to meet with a number of catechetical leaders from the surrounding Catholic parishes for a dialogue. He agreed and the catechetical leaders were excited to have an opportunity to participate in a positive interreligious experience.

A week before the meeting, the Imam called me and said that he regretted that he would not be able to attend, but that he would send a representative in his place. At the meeting, the catechetical leaders and I listened as this gracious gentleman explained the basic precepts of Islam in a very straightforward manner. When all was said and done, I thanked him for joining us and sharing his knowledge of Islam with us. I asked him what his position at the mosque was. He laughed and said, "Oh, no, I do not work at the Mosque. I own a video store on 95th Street!" I was flabbergasted, as were those standing nearby who overheard. We thought he was the Muslim equivalent of a catechetical leader or an associate pastor in a Catholic parish. In essence what had happened was the "pastor" (the Imam) had invited one of his "parishioners" to speak about Islam in his place!

Could you do the same if your pastor asked you to represent him at a meeting of non-Catholics who wanted to learn more about the Catholic faith?

I've asked this question to numerous groups of Catholics, especially catechists, and the number of people who feel they would have the right tools to represent the Catholic faith properly is extremely low. Why is this? Is the Catholic faith so complex that we cannot summarize it in some simple ways? Muslims can speak of the five pillars of Islam—the five duties required of every Muslim—and Buddhists can speak of the Four Noble Truths and the Eightfold Path.

So, what can Catholics speak of? For the answer to that, we can go to the four pillars of our Catholic faith, as outlined in the *Catechism of the Catholic Church.* If someone were to ask us to explain the Catholic faith to them, we should be able to turn to these four pillars—Creed, Sacraments, Morality, and Prayer—for guidance. When it comes to talking about our faith, these four pillars provide us with all of the H.E.L.P. that we need:

H = We *Hold* on to our faith that is revealed to us through Scripture and Tradition and is summarized in the Creed.

E = We *Express* our faith in the liturgy and sacraments of the Church.

L = We *Live* our faith according to Catholic morality.

P = We *Pray* our faith by maintaining a healthy prayer life.

With H.E.L.P., we should be able to do as St. Peter urged in his Letter: "Always be ready to give an explanation to anyone who asks you for a reason for your hope" (1 Peter 3:15).

A Well-Built Faith

I had the opportunity to watch a home being built right next door to mine. Over weeks and months, I saw a beautiful new home rise from its foundation to take its place as the biggest home on our block. It was a sight to see. Later, when folks moved in, I had a chance to talk to my new neighbor and compliment him on his beautiful new home. Surprisingly, he launched into a litany of complaints about how poorly the home was built. While beautiful from the outside, it seems the home was not well built and was now creating a number of headaches for the new owner.

When it comes to our faith, it needs to be well built, not just attractive looking from the outside. This book, *A Well-Built Faith,* is designed to give you H.E.L.P. so that you have a firm foundation to speak about your faith. Ongoing faith formation is an action that says, in essence, "God is so great, so wonderful, and so loving, that with every fiber of my being, I want to know him more intimately." God is actively present in our lives, shaping us into the person that reflects his divine image. Learning about our faith is not simply an intellectual exercise. It is a movement of the heart. St. Anselm taught that theology can be thought of as "faith seeking understanding." We seek to understand the Lord God so that our faith may be strengthened and, like St. Richard of Chichester, we may be able to "see thee more clearly, love thee more dearly, and follow thee more nearly . . . day by day." With a well-built faith, we can do this.

Ash Wednesday, 2008

PART ONE

The Creed:
Holding on to Faith

Chapter One

Laying a Firm Foundation: Transmitting Faith

I love working with cement and concrete. I suppose that goes back to when I was a boy. One of my favorite things was to watch a cement truck at a construction site. What little boy is not amazed by the pouring of wet cement? At the same time, what little boy can resist immortalizing himself by etching his initials in wet cement? Not that I ever did that, of course. By the way, if you find the initials J.P. in the foundation of your home, it's probably my brother, John. Anyway, when it comes to our faith, it is important to have a firm foundation. Luckily, the Catholic faith is founded on four pillars.

"Christians are made, not born."
—Tertullian, Church Father, third century AD

Making Christians

In the second century, one of the Church Fathers—Tertullian—wrote that "Christians are made, not born." Tertullian was reminding us that it is the Church's responsibility to make Christians and that this task involves certain tools used in a certain way. Tertullian, of course, was merely reminding us of what Jesus said right before his Ascension into heaven: "Go, therefore, and make disciples of all nations, baptizing them in the name of the Father, and of the Son, and of the holy Spirit, teaching them to observe all that I have commanded you" (Matthew 28:19–20). Jesus is quite clear that making

disciples is our great commission and he gives us an indication of how we are to do this: by baptizing and by teaching.

Jesus himself identified what is needed for a firm foundation in the Christian life—faith, hope, love, forgiveness, compassion, mercy, justice, and so on—but he didn't stop there. He showed us, through his own life example, how this firm foundation is built and strengthened. This task of building faith and making disciples of Christ is known as *evangelization.* And it is the Church's most important task. Pope Paul VI said this boldly in his encyclical *On Evangelization in the Modern World*, "The Church exists in order to evangelize." To evangelize is to call people to conversion—to call people from following misguided paths to following Jesus who is the Way, the Truth, and the Life. To make a Christian is to impart a way of life. This means that becoming a follower of Jesus—a disciple—requires not only *information* but also *transformation.* We need to *know* certain things to be a disciple of Jesus, but we also need to *do* specific things to live as his followers.

Following Jesus requires not only *information* but *transformation.*

Beginning with the End in Mind

When you build something, it's always good to begin with the end in mind.

When it comes to forming Catholics in faith, we, too, should begin with the end in mind.

So, just what is an adult Catholic supposed to "look like"? The answer very simply is: we are all to become saints.

"The Church offers to all people the possibility of encountering the living God today and finding in him lasting meaning and hope."

(*USCC for Adults*, p. 499)

Of course, few if any of us will ever be canonized as saints. However, the church has always had another understanding of the word *saints.* The early church referred to all of the faithful followers of Jesus as *the saints.* And how did the saints live? "They devoted themselves to the teaching of the apostles and to the communal life, to the breaking of the bread and to the prayers" (Acts of the Apostles 2:42). In other words, the saints—the first followers of Jesus—devoted themselves to the following:

- **holding on to their faith**
- **expressing faith**
- **living faith**
- **praying faith**

These are the four "pillars" of our Catholic way of life, then and now.

Laying a Firm Foundation — Understanding the Four Pillars of Our Faith

When someone makes an argument that has little or no substance to it, we say that the person "doesn't have a leg to stand on." As Catholics, we actually have *four* legs to stand on! The *Catechism of the Catholic Church* teaches us that our faith is grounded in the firm foundation of the following four principles:

1. **the Creed (holding on to faith)**
2. **the sacraments (expressing faith)**
3. **the moral life (living faith)**
4. **prayer (praying faith)**

The Four Pillars of Every Relationship

Every loving relationship includes the following four principles:

1. You love that person because you *believe* certain things about him or her to be true: he or she is good, kind, forgiving, fun to be with, or any number of other qualities.
2. You *express* your love for that person in a variety of ways: cards, flowers, gifts, hugs, kisses, a gentle touch, a passionate embrace.
3. You *act* toward that person in a way that shows you love and respect him or her.
4. You *communicate* with that person in an ongoing manner, even if separated by distance.

In a similar way, each of us has been baptized into a deep, intimate, and loving relationship with God and with one another. This relationship is supported by

- what we believe about God (the Creed)
- how we express our love for God and how God expresses his love for us (the sacraments)
- how we act toward God and toward others (the moral life)
- how we communicate with God (prayer)

The Creed (Holding on to Faith)

Believing is something that we do, not only with our heads, but also with our hearts. The following story illustrates this.

> A stunt man was thrilling crowds gathered at the Niagara Falls, making his way across a tightrope that stretched from one end of the Falls to the other while riding a unicycle and carrying another person on his shoulders! As he and his passenger successfully dismounted on solid ground, the crowd broke into wild applause. The stunt man thanked the crowd and asked, "How many of you truly believe that I can do that again?" Having just witnessed the amazing stunt, everyone in the crowd raised their hand. The stunt man then mounted his unicycle and pointed to his shoulders asking, "Alright, then, who's next?"

To believe is to enter into a relationship with another and to place our trust in that person. Until that happens, what we have is not a belief, but an idea. An idea evolves into a belief when it makes the leap from the head to the heart. Belief or faith is not blind. It is grounded in reason. We do not intimately love another person unless we have good reason (and some degree of evidence) to think that this person can be trusted. In the same way, we place our faith in God, not blindly, but based on good reason and some degree of evidence that God can be trusted. What is that evidence? Namely, the story of salvation history and the living witness of other followers of Christ. The Sacred Scriptures tell us the story of how God has been faithful to his people since the dawn of creation. The living witness of the saints—those canonized and those quietly leading lives of faith—provides us with credible evidence of the trustworthiness of God. Our own experience can also lead us to believe that God can be trusted. And yet, in the end, we have no proof, no guarantee—only an invitation to trust. And so, when we say in the Creed, "We believe in one God," we do so at our own risk.

Belief or faith is not blind. It is grounded in reason.

The Sacraments (Expressing Faith)

To be sacramental is to express beyond words. Catholics are sacramental because human beings are sacramental. Humans express love in a variety of ways beyond words. We do not feel that our love is fully expressed unless we can reach out to another person and touch them in some way. We are bodily creatures who experience the spiritual world in bodily—physical—ways. And so, as Catholics, we experience God and express ourselves to God using the physical. We use our bodies (standing, kneeling, bowing, lifting hands, signing ourselves) and we use physical objects (water, oil, bread, wine, fire, garments, rosary beads, incense) to encounter God who transcends words. We worship the intangible God using tangible realities.

The Moral Life (Living Faith)

Country and Western songs tend to be filled with heartache, telling tales of good loving gone bad. Two people in love are supposed to treat each other in a certain way and when that doesn't happen, relationships lose faith. Just as certain actions express that love, other actions express rejection of that love.

God is in love with us and he is inviting us to love him and one another in return. If we say that we love God, then we are supposed to act in ways that express that love and avoid actions that show rejection of that love. It's that simple.

Then why is it so hard?

It seems like living a moral life should be so easy. There are only ten rules to follow (the Commandments), and God is so wonderful and loving, who would ever dream of doing wrong by him? The painful truth is, we human beings are never satisfied. We always want more. Our hungry hearts seek satisfaction in places and things other than God. Like a married person who seems to "have it all" but still goes off to have an affair, we can all too easily forget how good God is to us and instead, go off to seek fulfillment elsewhere.

Marvin and Tina were not a very religious couple but tried their best; they only went to church once a year. As they were leaving the church, the priest said, "Marvin, it sure would be nice to see you and Tina at Mass more than once a year." "I know," replied Marvin, "We're very busy people, leading active lives, but at least we keep the Ten Commandments." "That's great," the priest said. "I'm glad to hear that you keep the Commandments." "Yes, we sure do," Marvin said proudly. "Tina keeps six of them and I keep the other four."

Living the moral life is not a matter of simply avoiding bad things. It is a matter of recognizing how loved we are and then responding to that love in the way our beloved—God—asks us to: by seeking fulfillment only in him and by loving our neighbors. God is faithful to us and we cannot hurt God through our immoral actions. The only hearts that risk becoming "achey-breaky" are our own.

Prayer (Praying Faith)

A survey conducted years ago asked people in successful marriages to identify the top ten qualities of a healthy marriage. One might think that sex, given all the attention it is given in our culture, would have been the number one quality. Not so. What was number one? *Communication!* Relationships last when people communicate with one another.

Prayer is the way we communicate with God. Communication, of course, is a two-way street: speaking and listening. Many of us were taught that prayer is "talking to God." This is only part of the dynamic of prayer. If prayer were understood as simply talking to God, than St. Paul's insistence that we should "pray always" would mean that we should be talking incessantly to God. Poor God! Imagine having to listen to someone else speak incessantly! Without listening, we are missing the voice of God. Later on in this book, we'll explore how God speaks to us and what it means to *hear* God's voice. For now, it is enough to know that prayer is the fourth pillar of our Catholic faith and that without prayer we run the risk of collapsing like a card table with only three legs.

> **"The goal of the *Catechism of the Catholic Church* is to help facilitate the lifelong conversion of the whole person to the Father's call to holiness and eternal life."**
>
> (*USCC for Adults*, p. xvii)

So What?

What difference does it make for Catholics to believe that "Christians are made, not born"? It means that we are called to be receptive. Faith is something that we *receive.* It does not belong to us but is passed on to us like a family heirloom that we treasure, protect, and pass on faithfully. To be receptive means to think of God as the potter and ourselves as the clay. God, through the Church, forms us. The clay doesn't tell the potter how it wants to be shaped.

Scripture

"Go therefore, and make disciples of all nations, baptizing them in the name of the Father, and of the Son, and of the holy Spirit, teaching them to observe all that I have commanded you. And behold, I am with you always, until the end of the age." (MATTHEW 28:18–20)

Prayer

Lord God, each day is another opportunity for you to make me into one of your disciples. If I have failed you recently, remake me, so that I may hold on to my faith in you, express my faith in you, live that faith, and pray from within that faith. And thank you for being with me, always! Amen.

Chapter Two

Assembly-Line Construction: Human Desire, Revelation, and Faith

Many things that we rely on in our day-to-day lives are constructed or manufactured on assembly lines. Probably the most familiar example is an automobile assembly line. Every worker on the line contributes to the product as it moves along. By the time the product reaches a worker on the line, it has already been "started" by someone else. Assembly line workers are always working with what someone else has given them. The same is true in our faith lives. We are not building from scratch. God has begun the process and now invites us to share and participate in his creation.

Looking for Love

Speed dating has grown in popularity among young adults in recent years. How does it work? Basically, young men and women gather at a bar or restaurant and rotate every three to five minutes, briefly interviewing one another in hopes of finding a match. During their short time together, each person tries to reveal something about himself or herself to make an impression upon the other, in hopes of getting a date. When the process ends, the women can indicate which of the men they would like to arrange a date with.

Why do people do this? Because they are looking for a relationship. Relationships are formed when people reveal themselves to one another. Granted, three to five minutes is not a lot of time to adequately reveal the essence of one's being or to establish trust. However, when people feel that something unique and attractive about another person has been revealed, they are drawn to enter into a relationship with that person. In a relationship, both parties hope to reveal and discover—and ultimately to love.

When it comes down to it, the Catholic faith is all about *relationship.* God passionately seeks to enter into a deep and intimate relationship with each one of us. To that end, God reveals himself to us. Although God already knows each of us intimately, we need to come to know God. Since the dawn of creation, God has been revealing himself, inviting men and women throughout the ages to enter into relationship with him. We call this act of God's self-revealing *revelation.*

"God wants to speak to you. Consult your local listings."

This may come as a surprise. *Revelation* is often thought of as some type of mystical experience reserved for selected prophets, saints, and visionaries. However, revelation simply refers to the act of God revealing himself to us in order to enter into a deeper relationship with us. The key is that God is the one taking the initiative. We sometimes think that we have come to the decision to deepen our relationship with God . . . to become more spiritual . . . to "get religion." The fact is, when we do these things, we are responding to God's invitation. God started it.

Revelation is the self-disclosure of the living God.
(*USCC for Adults,* p. 13)

There's No Such Thing as Being Spiritually Proactive

In his book, *The Seven Habits of Highly Effective People* (Free Press, 1990), Stephen Covey identifies being proactive as one of the seven habits, encouraging us to be proactive in our careers and in our relationships. This type of thinking often carries over into our spiritual lives. We will take the initiative to pray more, to live a more virtuous life, and to practice spiritual disciplines. These are indeed good things, however, there is one problem with this type of thinking: it creates the illusion that WE are the ones being proactive—as if our own efforts will somehow grab God's attention.

The Scriptures are filled with stories of people trying to be spiritually proactive.

- **Adam and Eve decided that they could be proactive and become god-like by eating of the tree of knowledge of good and evil.**
- **The folks who built the tower of Babel thought that they could be proactive in reaching the heavens (God's dwelling place) by building their skyscraper.**
- **Judas thought he could be proactive by precipitating a confrontation in which Jesus could reveal his power.**

God desires to have an intimate relationship with all people.
(*USCC for Adults*, p. 13)

Needless to say, none of these stories turned out well for those who thought they could be proactive with God. Instead, we turn to examples of people throughout Scripture who responded to God's initiative.

- **Abraham and Sarah recognized that God was calling them to a new life and they responded by uprooting themselves and moving to a strange land.**
- **Moses recognized God's presence in a burning bush and responded to God's invitation to lead his people out of slavery.**
- **Mary responded to God's messenger, the angel Gabriel, by accepting God's invitation to become the mother of his Son.**

A scientist decided to take the initiative and create human life from scratch. He called out to God and said, "God, we no longer need you. Science has developed to the point where we can create human beings without your initiative." God said, "Oh, is that so? Let's have a human being making contest, but we have to agree to do this just like I did back in the old days with Adam and Eve." "Sure," replied the scientist, who then bent down and grabbed himself a handful of dirt to get started. God interrupted him with a smile and said, "Oh, no, you don't. You go make your own dirt!"

God Started It—And They Responded

Take a look at these examples from Scripture to see how God initiated the invitation and how folks responded.

- Genesis 12:1-9 (the call of Abram)
- Exodus 3: 1-14 (the call of Moses)
- Isaiah 6:1-10 (the call of Isaiah)
- Jeremiah 1:4-10 (the call of Jeremiah)
- Matthew 5:18-22 (the call of the first disciples)
- Luke 1: 26-38 (the call of Mary)
- Acts of the Apostles 9:1-9 (the call of Paul)

The central thread of Sacred Scripture is God's unrelenting pursuit of his people and the challenge for his people to respond to God's invitation. This same dynamic holds true for us today. We simply cannot be spiritually proactive. God has already taken the first step. Since the moment of our birth, God has been pursuing us, seeking us out, and inviting us to a deeper relationship with him. The saints were not people who were spiritually proactive. Rather, they were people who were highly responsive to God's invitation. Understanding this dynamic is crucial, because it enables us to place the spiritual horse before the spiritual cart, so to speak. Instead of making it our responsibility to pursue God, we can turn our attention to God's pursuit of us—his revelation—and seek proper ways to respond. Like working on an assembly line, we don't start from scratch. God started it.

Thy Will Be Done

Of course, Jesus' entire life is a portrait of how to respond to God. In the musical *Jesus Christ Superstar,* there is a poignant scene in the Garden of

"Couldn't I talk to a burning bush of something?"

Gethsemane in which the character of Jesus prays to his heavenly Father about his impending death.

> After all I've tried for three years seems like ninety
> Why then am I scared to finish what I started
> What you started—I didn't start it

There are two kinds of people: those who say to God, "Thy will be done," and those to whom God says, "All right, then, have it your way."
—C. S. Lewis

The character of Jesus comes to the realization that it is not of his own doing that he has come to this moment, but is a result of following his Father's will. It is only after this realization that the character of Jesus is able to utter the words, "still, not my will but yours be done" (Luke 22:42). When we recognize that God is the initiator, the instigator, the proactive One, we come to realize that our task in life is to discern God's will and to respond as Jesus did, "thy will be done."

Humility

Understanding the dynamic of *revelation*—that God has taken the initiative to reveal himself to us in hopes of entering into a loving relationship—is the first step toward living a life of *humility*. Why? Because it is the first step in realizing that "it's not about us"—it's about God and what God is doing in our lives. Revelation is about God revealing himself, drawing attention to himself, so that we might come to recognize him more clearly and respond. Saints are not people who draw attention to themselves, but to God.

John the Baptist said, "He must increase; I must decrease" (John 3:30).

IT'S NOT ABOUT YOU!

Today, we live in a society that tells us in a variety of ways that, "it's all about you!" Revelation is God's not-so-gentle reminder that "it's not about you . . . it's about what I (God) am doing in your life." For many of us, this is a *Copernican revolution*. Remember Copernicus? He was the Polish astronomer and mathematician who proposed that the earth revolved around the sun and not the other way around. For us, revelation is God's way of reminding us that our lives revolve around him, not the other way around.

Mary said, "My soul proclaims the greatness of the Lord" (Luke 1:46).

St. Ignatius of Loyola taught his followers, the Jesuits, to do all things *ad majorem dei gloriam*—for the greater glory of God.

The deepening of one's spiritual life is not so much the arduous climbing toward the peak of a very high mountain, but rather the hoisting of a sail to catch the wind that will draw us to another destination. In the spiritual life, the best we can do is to conspire with God. It's time we stopped thinking that we can paddle ourselves across the great sea of life and, instead, determine which way the spirit is blowing and hoist our sails, allowing ourselves to be guided to distant shores.

So What?

What difference does it make for Catholics to believe in *revelation*? It means that we are to be *aware* and *responsive* to God's initiative. Since God's very self has been and is being revealed to us, it means that we are called to pay attention to how and when that is happening so that we become capable of, as St. Ignatius of Loyola said, "finding God in all things." It means that we are called to respond to God's revealing of himself to us, aware that we are not trying to get God's attention but are responding to God's efforts to get our attention.

Scripture

Meanwhile Moses was tending the flock of his father-in-law Jethro, the priest of Midian. Leading the flock across the desert, he came to Horeb, the mountain of God. There an angel of the LORD appeared to him in fire flaming out of a bush. When the LORD saw him coming over to look at it more closely, God called out to him from the bush, "Moses! Moses!" He answered, "Here I am." (EXODUS 3:1–2, 4)

Prayer

Lord, God, since before I was born, you have been longing to be in relationship with me. Help me to recognize the many ways you are revealing yourself to me and calling my name. Help me to respond to your invitation to love you by loving others. Please give me the grace I need to pray the words "your will be done."

Chapter Three

Who's the Boss?: Scripture and Tradition

Any construction site requires a foreman—someone with the authority to direct the job and all of the workers on that job. Workers need to know who is in charge and to whom they can turn to find direction and clarification. Authority is an important issue in matters of faith as well. To place faith in someone is to recognize their authority in certain matters. To have faith in God is to recognize God's authority over all things and all people.

"Says Who?"

As kids, we didn't like it when someone we considered to be an equal assumed authority over us. We challenged their authority by asking, "Says who?" We wanted to know where this authority was coming from. If, indeed, they were able to point to another authority (e.g., "Says Mom" or "Says our teacher"), we immediately wanted to know when, where, and to whom these words of authority were spoken.

Jesus spoke with authority. Of course, many people resented that. They had assumed that Jesus was their equal. They asked on more than one occasion from where Jesus was getting his authority. In other words, they were asking, "Says who?" Jesus made it very clear where his authority came from: "All power in heaven and on earth has been given to me" (Matthew 28:18). This means, of course, that Jesus speaks with the authority of God. Jesus, in turn, gave this authority to his Church when he told Peter that he would build his church upon him and gave him the keys of the kingdom (Matthew 16:18–19).

To be entrusted with the keys to anything is to be given authority. So, when Christians preach the Gospel with authority, people, in essence, ask, "Says who?" They want to know where our authority comes from. Our answer, very simply, is God, from whom all authority comes. Of course, the next question that follows is, "where, when, and to whom did God say that?" Protestants and Catholics answer this question differently. For Protestants, the answer is, "in the Bible." Having separated from the Roman Catholic Church in the sixteenth century and distrusting of church hierarchy, Protestantism claimed that God's revelation is found only in Scripture. For Catholics, the source of authority—the source of God's revelation—is Scripture *and* Tradition. Let's take a closer look at these.

For Catholics, the source of authority—the source of God's revelation—is Scripture *and* Tradition.

The pinnacle of God's revelation is, of course, Jesus Christ. Jesus speaks and acts with the authority of God because he *is* God. Jesus, in turn, commissioned his apostles to carry on his mission and sent his Holy Spirit to be with the Church. So, we can visualize the issue of authority this way:

God has all authority

God has given all authority to his Son, Jesus Christ

Jesus has given authority to the Church,
through Peter and his successors

Throughout the ages, the bishops, the successors of the apostles, have passed on the Word of God with the guidance of the Holy Spirit. The Word of God takes the form of both the written word (Scripture) and of a living Tradition. Both, however, have as their source, Jesus Christ. In other words, Catholics know that Scripture alone is not enough. We also need (and have) authoritative

Tradition is the living transmission of the message of the Gospel in the Church.
(*USCC for Adults*, p. 25)

interpretation and teaching. For Catholics, Scripture and Tradition are inseparable, forming one "sacred deposit of the Word of God" (*Catechism of the Catholic Church*, 97).

Tradition, in this context, is not just the act of doing something a certain way because "that's how it's always been done." Tradition is the faithful handing on of the teaching of the apostles under the guidance of the Holy Spirit. This responsibility for a faithful handing on of the teaching of the apostles belongs to the Magisterium—the teaching office of the Church.

Which Came First, Scripture or Tradition?

Some people like to think that the Bible is the final word on all matters. There's only one problem with that. The Bible, as we know it today, is the product of Tradition. In other words, an oral tradition of preaching the Gospel existed before the New Testament was written down. Likewise, the final arrangement of the books of the Bible as we have it today was set in place by the leaders of the early Church. The Bible, which flows from Church Tradition, is part of a single source of God's revelation. It is the revealed Word of God.

Here's some basic information about the Bible.

- **The Catholic Bible is made up of seventy-three books.**
- **There are forty-six books in the Old Testament.**
- **There are twenty-seven books in the New Testament.**
- **Protestant Bibles have only sixty-six books. They recognize only thirty-nine books in the Old Testament, leaving out Tobit, Judith, 1 and 2 Maccabees, Wisdom, Sirach, and Baruch.**
- **The Old Testament is the story of the people of Israel before the birth of Jesus Christ.**

What's a Magisterium?

In Latin, the word for teacher or master is *magister*. It is the role of the bishops, the successors of Peter, to teach as Jesus commanded. When talking about the teaching authority of the Church, we use the term *Magisterium*, referring to the bishops—our teachers—in communion with the pope and under the guidance of the Holy Spirit. We rely on the Magisterium to authentically teach and interpret the truths of our faith.

Tradition!

When speaking of Tradition, it's hard not to think of Tevye from the musical *A Fiddler on the Roof* who, in the opening scenes, speaks proudly about the role of tradition in his home town of Anatevka, but can't explain a single one. That's not quite the Catholic understanding of Tradition. Tevye is actually referring to traditions—doing certain things the same way over and over again. Catholics have traditions. But we also have Tradition—a living body of teaching that is passed on and preserved with faithfulness, responding with newness to the unique circumstances of each generation and culture it comes into contact with.

⊕ **The Old Testament includes the following sections:**

Pentateuch (*Torah,* in Jewish tradition): The first five books of the Old Testament tell the story of the beginnings of the relationship between God and the people of Israel with the central focus being the Exodus event—the experience of being led from slavery to freedom.

History: The Books of Joshua through Second Maccabees record the stories of the people of Israel who, under various leaders (judges and kings), fought to enter and keep the Promised Land, a struggle that continues to this day.

Wisdom: The Books of Job through Sirach gather together all the wisdom teachings of the people of Israel that were collected over thousands of years. While the Psalms are not technically considered Wisdom Literature (they are more appropriately liturgical hymns), Psalms traditionally have been placed with the Wisdom books.

A little boy opened the big family Bible with fascination and looked at the old pages as he turned them. Suddenly, something fell out of the Bible. He picked it up and looked at it closely. It was an old leaf from a tree that had been pressed between the pages. "Momma, look what I found," the boy called out. "What have you got there, dear?" his mother asked. With excitement, the young boy answered: "I think it's Adam's suit!"

Prophets: The Books of Isaiah through Malachi describe how the Prophets called the people of Israel to be faithful to the Covenant.

The New Testament is the story of the Christian experience, beginning with the life of Jesus Christ and continuing with the early church.

The Gospels: Comprised of accounts from Matthew, Mark, Luke, and John, the Gospels contain the stories of the life, teachings, miracles, passion, death, and resurrection of Jesus of Nazareth.

"Ignorance of Scripture is ignorance of Christ."
—St. Jerome

Acts of the Apostles: This book, which is a "sequel" to Luke's Gospel, retells the experience of the early Christian community, beginning with Jesus' Ascension into heaven and leading up to Paul's arrival in Rome.

Letters: Also known as the Epistles, the Letters—Romans through Jude—represent the communications of the early church. They are designed to teach, admonish, encourage, correct, and update the various churches.

Revelation: The last book of the Bible is highly misunderstood because of its use of many symbols and figurative language to describe the eternal struggle between good and evil. Despite all of the frightening imagery, the uplifting conclusion of this book is that good has and will always prevail.

How Do Catholics Interpret the Bible?

The essence of the Catholic approach to understanding the Bible can be summed up this way: everything in the Bible is *true* . . . but not necessarily *fact*. This statement is not meant to be tricky or gimmicky. Rather, it points out that truth and fact are not always the same thing. We can say that it is "raining cats and dogs" to communicate truth without using facts. We call this figurative language. There are parts of the Bible, especially in the Old Testament, that rely on figurative language to express God's truth. Catholics believe in the inerrancy of the Bible, meaning that the Bible makes no mistakes when it comes to communicating the absolute *truth* of God. At the same time, the Bible is not always accurate when relating *facts*. The creation stories in Genesis are not intended to teach scientific facts about the beginnings of the universe. They are however true stories, teaching us the absolute essential truth about God's relationship with all of creation:

- **God is the author of all things and of all life.**
- **Human beings are made in the divine image.**
- **God brought order out of chaos.**
- **All of creation is good.**
- **Humankind has been given dominion (stewardship) over the earth's resources.**

Catholics do not have to choose between creationism on the one hand and Darwin's theory of evolution on the other. We recognize that the Bible teaches religious truth and that science teaches scientific truth. We need both, and we see no conflict between faith and science. Simply put, Catholics believe that the Bible is the Word of God and everything in it is true. We simply do not take every line of the Bible literally. (To learn more about how Catholics understand the Bible, see my book *God's Library: A Catholic Introduction to the World's Greatest Book,* Loyola Press.)

Tradition and Decision Making

When Catholics are seeking guidance from God's Word, we can turn to the Bible. However, we also can consult Church Tradition. How do we do that? It means that we look to the Magisterium—the teaching authority of the Church—for guidance. For those who teach the Catholic faith, the best way to consult the Tradition of the Church is to turn to the *Catechism of the Catholic Church.* For those who are simply trying to live the Catholic faith day to day, a good place to turn to is the *United States Catholic Catechism for Adults,* which I quote throughout this book. We are blessed as Catholics to not only have the Bible to guide us, but to be able to look to what the Church, under the guidance of the Holy Spirit, has taught through ecumenical councils, papal encyclicals, pastoral letters, and other official sources of teachings from our bishops.

So What?

So what difference does it make that Catholics believe that the sources of God's revelation are *Scripture* and *Tradition*? It means that we don't walk around pretending to have all of the answers in a book. It means that we recognize the movement of the Holy Spirit guiding us as a Church to find the truth through the Word of God that comes to us in a living Tradition.

Scripture

But you, remain faithful to what you have learned and believed, because you know from whom you learned it, and that from infancy you have known (the) sacred scriptures, which are capable of giving you wisdom for salvation through faith in Christ Jesus. All scripture is inspired by God and is useful for teaching, for refutation, for correction, and for training in righteousness, so that one who belongs to God may be competent, equipped for every good work. (2 TIMOTHY 3:14–17)

Prayer

Holy Spirit, guide us to encounter the Living God, revealed to us in Scripture and Tradition. Help us to receive God's Word, passed on to us through this one deposit of faith—Scripture and Tradition—and to be nourished by it so that we, in turn, may pass it along to others.

Chapter Four

Using Brand-Name Equipment: The Trinity

When selecting tools for construction jobs, there are many brand names to choose from: Black & Decker, Craftsman, Makita, Stanley, and so on. What's in a name? I used to think, nothing. I prided myself in purchasing tools on the cheap. Of course, you get what you pay for. Now, I use only brand name tools. I like to know who I'm working with. In matters of faith, it is important to know with whose name we are associated. As Catholics, we announce it loud and clear that we do all things in the name of the Father, and of the Son, and of the Holy Spirit.

You Look Just Like Your . . .

To whom do you most bear a family resemblance? Mom? Dad? Grandmother or grandfather? Brother or sister? Aunt or uncle? Many of us can be identified as members of a family by our physical and personality traits. Now, think about this one: "Do you bear a family resemblance to your Father in heaven?" The Book of Genesis tells us that God created us, male and female, in the Divine image. So, just what is our image of God and how do we "resemble" him? Of course, we're not talking about physical characteristics, because God transcends the physical realm. However, being made in the image and likeness of God means that we bear qualities that are God-like.

Being made in the image and likeness of God means that we bear qualities that are God-like.

The Creed, the first pillar of our faith, makes it very clear that we believe in God who is Father, Son, and Holy Spirit. In other words, the Christian image of God is Trinitarian—that is, we believe in the Trinity—one God, three persons. We are baptized "In the name of the Father, and of the Son, and of the Holy Spirit." The Trinity is our "brand name."

The Trinity Is a Mystery

Now, if you ask most people to explain the Trinity, they will respond by saying, "Well, it's a mystery of faith. We just have to accept it." In other words, "I don't understand the Trinity. Never have and never will." This disclaimer is usually preceded by feeble attempts to compare the reality of the Trinity to a three-leaf clover. However well-intentioned, these approaches to talking about the Trinity miss the profound depths of our understanding of God and how we can and do reflect that image in our everyday lives.

The mystery of the Most Holy Trinity is the central mystery of the Christian faith and life.

(*USCC for Adults*, p. 52)

Interestingly enough, our faith teaches us that the doctrine of the Trinity is the "central mystery of Christian faith and life" (*General Directory for Catechesis,* 99), and that this doctrine has "vital implications for the lives of human beings" (*General Directory for Catechesis,* 100). Wow. Guess that means that this is a doctrine worth spending some time on.

We shouldn't be afraid of doctrine, which is intended to illuminate our understanding of God. Doctrine is not intended for theologians. It's intended to help everyday people come closer to God through a deeper understanding of the truths that God has revealed to us. The doctrine of the Trinity, then, is not something intended to befuddle us or to be dismissed by us as a mystery never to be understood. In matters of faith, *mystery* is something that can be "known," even if not fully understood. We can most definitely know the Trinity, even if we do not fully understand the reality of Three Persons in One God.

The doctrine of the Trinity was not developed by theologians. It came about from the lives of the early Christians as they encountered the Father, in Jesus and through the Holy Spirit. Unfortunately, as the centuries progressed the concept of the Trinity evolved into an abstract theological formula that became seemingly irrelevant to Christian living. Eventually,

Unfortunately, as the centuries progressed, the concept of the Trinity evolved into an abstract theological formula that became irrelevant to Christian living.

people began to see God as a distant supreme being who needs to battle other lesser beings to get our attention. As a result, people did not see God as someone who was intimately involved in our everyday living. They saw life more as profane and godless, except for those occasional moments when God intervened.

God Is Love

How unfortunate that people have come to see God as a distant supreme being. A closer look at our Creed reveals a much different understanding of God. In the Nicene Creed, we say that we believe that Jesus is "one in being with the Father" and that the Holy Spirit, "proceeds from the Father and the Son." This means that we understand God, not as an individual but as a community of love. In other words, God's very essence is loving relationship. When we say that God is love, something we teach to the littlest of children, we are recalling the love that exists between Father, Son, and Holy Spirit. This is why love of neighbor is so critical in Christianity: because loving relationship is the very essence of God and we most reflect the image of God when we live in loving relationship with our neighbors. In fact, God does not just have a loving relationship—God *is* loving relationship. Love is not just a trait of God but is the very essence of God.

NO SUPREME BEING?

Did you know that Catholics do not believe in a supreme being? Truth is, we don't believe that God is a distant supreme being; we don't believe that God is a supreme being at all. A supreme being is a being that is simply superior to other beings. God is the Creator of human beings. God is not a being, but is the very ground of being—the very essence of being. So, what is God, if not a being? God is God. That's why he told Moses, "I Am who Am." In other words, God just is.

Jesus said, "Who do people say that I am?" And his disciples answered, "Some say you are John the Baptist returned from the dead; others say Elijah or one of the other prophets." And Jesus answered, "But who do you say that I am?" Peter answered, "Thou art the Logos, existing in the Father as His rationality and then, by an act of His will, being generated, in consideration of the various functions by which God is related to his creation, but only on the fact that Scripture speaks of a Father, and a Son, and a Holy Spirit, each member of the Trinity being coequal with every other member, and each acting inseparably with and interpenetrating every other member, with only an economic subordination within God, but causing no division which would make the substance no longer simple."

And Jesus answered, saying, "Huh?" (*loosely* adapted from Luke 9:18–21)

What does this all mean? It means that the Trinity—the Father, Son, and Holy Spirit in a loving relationship—is the most perfect expression of who God is and how God is present and active in this world. As beings made in the image and likeness of God and baptized in the name of the Father, Son, and Holy Spirit, our truest identity is to be in communion with one another and with God. It is our human nature to seek intimacy with others. Even when we are hurt by others, we eventually find ourselves, after a time of healing, once again seeking relationships. When we give over to this desire to be in relationship, we are sharing in the life of God who is love.

This is why Catholics consider it folly when people say that they are spiritual, but not religious—meaning that they love God, but can do without worship that involves community. For Catholics, communion with God is inseparable from communion with others. And our communion with others is not reserved to other Catholics. Since we believe that all human beings are made in the image and likeness of God, we are called to be in communion—in relationship—with all people. The Catholic Church is a sign of the communion that all of humanity is called to. This means that the Church exists, not as an exclusive club, but as a vehicle for drawing all people into communion with God and one another.

For Catholics, communion with God is inseparable from communion with others.

As followers of Jesus, baptized in the name of the Trinity, we are called to live a life of communion, inviting others to recognize how God is intimately involved in their daily living. In essence, we help others to see God—Father, Son, and Holy Spirit—present and active in their daily experiences. We help them to see that every time they sacrifice their own personal desires in order to tend to the needs of another, they are experiencing and participating in the life of the Trinity.

Our belief in the Trinity also calls us to speak out against those things that interfere with peoples' ability to live in loving relationship with one another: poverty, drug and alcohol abuse, racial prejudice, and other injustices. This same belief calls us to tend to the needs of those whose suffering interferes with human relationships: the sick, the oppressed, the unemployed, the divorced, the grieving. We do all of these things because we bear a family resemblance to the Trinity—a community of loving relationship. To be baptized in the name of the Father, Son, and Holy Spirit, is to be wholly committed to living in solidarity with others. When we do so, we reflect the image of the Trinitarian God, whose essence is communion.

Our belief in the Trinity is not an intellectual exercise—it is a relationship. To say that we believe in the Trinity is not to try to explain some complex theological concept, but is to say that we are loved by the Father, the Creator of all things; by the Son, Jesus, the Redeemer; and by the Holy Spirit, the sanctifier and sustainer of life. You don't have to have the brilliance of a university professor or an IQ of 200 to know the Trinity. If you know that you are loved by God—who creates you, redeems you, and sustains you—then you *know* the Trinity.

So What?

So, what difference does it make that Catholics believe in the Trinity? It means that we believe that God is, in essence, loving relationship, and, since we are made in the image and likeness of God, it is our very nature to live in loving relationship with one another. To live in loving relationship with others is to

Self-Giving Love

Whenever we offer self-giving love to others, we are sharing in the life of the Trinity. That means that the following moments in life are profoundly Trinitarian:

- When you wake up in the middle of the night to change your baby's diaper.
- When you take some time at work to help a fellow employee get a better grasp of his or her responsibilities.
- When you check up on a neighbor who has been having a difficult time.
- When you interrupt your favorite TV show to take a phone call from a friend or relative who is lonely.
- When you spend time helping your child with homework after a long day at work.
- When you buy a cup of hot coffee for a homeless person you encounter on your way to work.

share in the divine life of the Trinity. This also means that we have a name to live up to. I recall in grammar school being reminded by the nuns that I was a Paprocki, which was a highly respected name in the parish and in the community, and that I better live up to that name. Since we are baptized in the name of the Father, and of the Son, and of the Holy Spirit, we need to live up to the name of God, the Holy Trinity.

Scripture

After Jesus was baptized, he came up from the water and behold, the heavens were opened (for him), and he saw the Spirit of God descending like a dove (and) coming upon him. And a voice came from the heavens, saying, "This is my beloved Son, with whom I am well pleased." (MATTHEW 3:16–17)

Prayer

Glory Be to the Father, and to the Son, and to the Holy Spirit, as it was in the beginning, is now and ever shall be, world without end. Amen.

Chapter Five

The Bulldozer: Sin, Salvation, and the Cross of Jesus

I remember watching the house that I grew up in being demolished. Bulldozers easily broke through walls and columns that had held the building together for years. The structure had withstood decades of wind, rain, hail, snow, ice, and nine Paprocki kids who played baseball, football, hockey, and basketball within its confines. Now, the bulldozers broke through these barriers as if tearing through tissue paper. In our lives we encounter many barriers, and we can hurt ourselves spiritually thinking that we can break through all of them. It is only through the cross of Jesus that these barriers—death being the greatest—can be overcome. Like a bulldozer, the Cross of Jesus breaks through all barriers.

In Critical Condition

"It's a matter of life and death."

Those are very dramatic words. To tell someone that they are facing a matter of life and death is to identify the situation as critical. In medical terms, when someone is listed as *critical,* it means that there is an equal chance of the person dying or recovering.

So what do life and death have to do with our faith? Isn't faith just a choice that we make in life to seek inspiration from a particular tradition? Isn't it just like choosing what brand of software you want to use on your computer? What could faith possibly have to do with life and death?

Actually, everything.

In the book of Deuteronomy, God states the case very bluntly: "I have set before you life and death, the blessing and the curse. Choose life . . ." (Deuteronomy 30:19). Jesus echoed this when he said, "I came so that they might have life and have it more abundantly" (John 10:10). So, just what is all this talk about life and death?

The Book of Genesis gives us a clue. Out of selfless love, God gave Adam and Eve the gift of free will so that they could freely choose to share in his love and divine life. Of course, Adam and Eve, representing the first humans, chose to reject this love and seek fulfillment elsewhere. As a result, sin entered the world and along with it, suffering and death. Death, then, is the ultimate consequence of humankind's sinful choices. Thus, sin is not merely a weakness that we can overcome through our own efforts—because we cannot overcome death, which is the ultimate consequence of sin. This is not to suggest, however, that any one person's death is directly related to their own sinful actions. It means that humankind, as a whole, experiences death because we, as a whole, have chosen a condition in life that seeks fullness of life in places other than God. As a result, we need a savior—a redeemer.

> **"Fear defeats more people than any other one thing in the world."**
> (Ralph Waldo Emerson)

If this were not true, then why are people afraid of death? Throughout human history, death has been our greatest fear, because it has been seen as the end of all things; the cessation of life; our final demise.

That is, until Jesus came along.

ORIGINAL SIN

As a kid, I always thought it was unfair that the rest of us had to suffer the stain of original sin, all because of the blunders of Adam and Eve. As adults we realize that, in essence, Adam and Eve represent us. Original sin is the tendency to choose, as Adam and Eve chose, our own desires over the will of God. Because of original sin, we are powerless in the face of sin and its ultimate consequence—death. We can only be saved by the One who has conquered sin and death: Jesus Christ. In baptism, original sin is "washed away," meaning that in Jesus we have embraced the only means by which we can overcome our own desires and conform to the will of God.

Jesus Overcomes Our Greatest Fear

"Wait! Wait! He doesn't stay dead!"

When Jesus became human (we call this the Incarnation), he took on our human condition. Jesus was not God pretending to be human, nor was he human pretending to be God. He was not half-God, half-human. Jesus, without losing his divinity (he is "God from God, Light from Light, True God from True God"), became fully human ("he was born of the Virgin Mary and became man"). That means that Jesus entered into our sinful state. Like us, he faced temptation. Unlike us, however, Jesus triumphed over temptation and sin. Jesus also faced suffering and death ("he suffered under Pontius Pilate, was crucified, died, and was buried."). Jesus faced not just any death, but the horrible death of an innocent victim—public execution. However, Jesus' battle with sin and death did not end in defeat. God raised Jesus up ("on the third day, he rose again," in fulfillment of the Scriptures). Jesus, through his Resurrection, overcame death, that most ultimate consequence of sin. Jesus' Resurrection is the ultimate triumph, because now we know that death is not the end. In Jesus, death—our greatest fear—is overcome. Thus, we are saved because even death cannot separate us from the love of Christ Jesus.

As baptized followers of Jesus, we continue to face sin, temptation, suffering, and death. However, in Jesus, we know that all of these can and will be overcome. So we have no reason to fear. We are safe. We are saved. No doubt this is why the words *do not fear, fear not, be not afraid,* and other similar variations appear literally hundreds of times in the Bible. No doubt this is why Jesus' first words to the apostles after his Resurrection were, "Peace be with you" (John 20:19). They had nothing to fear.

> **"The name *Jesus* means 'God saves.'"**
> (*USCC for Adults*, p. 85)

This is the meaning of the song "We Shall Overcome," a popular anthem of the Civil Rights Movement of the 1960s. This song is not the sentiments of one group of people threatening to overcome another group of people. Rather, it expresses the fearlessness of all Christians who know that, because Jesus overcame sin and death, he can help us to overcome anything—even a seemingly insurmountable injustice.

We shall overcome
We shall overcome
We shall overcome some day!
Oh, deep in my heart, I do believe,
We shall overcome some day!

The Cross—Our Trophy

Because of Jesus' Resurrection, we can look upon the cross as a symbol of victory—God's trophy, so to speak. Just as a victorious team marches in a parade, hoisting their trophy for all to see, we Catholics march in parades—only we call them processions, and they are led by God's trophy, the cross of Jesus, hoisted for all to see. The message is loud and clear: if God can overcome even the torture and execution of his only Son, he can overcome anything. Thus we, as his children in baptism, are able to overcome anything through faith in him. It is with this in mind that we joyfully sing the words to the traditional hymn, "Lift High the Cross!"

Lift High the Cross

Refrain
Lift high the cross, the love of Christ proclaim,
Till all the world adore His sacred Name.

Led on their way by this triumphant sign,
The hosts of God in conquering ranks combine.

Each newborn servant of the Crucified
Bears on the brow the seal of Him Who died.

O Lord, once lifted on the glorious tree,
As Thou hast promised, draw the world to Thee.

So shall our song of triumph ever be:
Praise to the Crucified for victory.

The Cross and Despair

When people find themselves in the midst of crisis, they are on the threshold of either hope or despair; feelings that say the present crisis cannot and

What Do You Fear?

Surveys show that the most common fears are (not necessarily in order)

1. bugs, mice, snakes, bats
2. crowds/public speaking
3. flying
4. water
5. confined spaces
6. wasps and insects
7. heights
8. crossing bridges
9. thunder and lightning
10. death

will not be overcome. People of faith—people who can see that God can and will overcome everything—need to be present to provide assurance for those in despair. This is why we, as Catholics, make it such a priority to visit the sick, the elderly, shut-ins, and those who are experiencing grief over the loss of a loved one or a broken relationship. We do not strive to convince them of God's presence, or speak dismissively of their pain as though they are being silly for not believing that God will overcome. We simply express through our steadfast presence, and our confidence that they will get through their pain, that through the grace of God they shall overcome.

"We get our salvation the old fashioned way—we earn it."

An exasperated mother, whose son was always getting into mischief, finally asked him, "How do you expect to be saved and get to heaven?" The boy thought it over and said, "Well, I'll run in and out and keep slamming the door until St. Peter says, 'For Heaven's sake, young man, come in or stay out!'"

Born-Again Catholics

The next time an evangelical Christian asks if you are saved, you can reply with confidence, "Absolutely. I believe in Jesus, who overcame death, and if he can overcome death, he can overcome anything." With Jesus, we are safe. Through Jesus, we are saved. Because we are saved, we have a share in eternal life. We no longer see death as the end, but as a transition. Salvation in Jesus is not a guarantee—it is a gift. The only way to embrace salvation is to embrace the suffering, death, and resurrection of Jesus. This means that we constantly strive to die to sin and live as a new creation, performing good works in response to this great gift. To reject the Resurrection is to reject hope. To reject hope is to have no future. To have no future is to have death. Faith in Jesus truly is a matter of life and death.

Faith in Jesus truly is a matter of life and death.

So What?

So what difference does it make that Catholics believe in the Cross of Jesus? Without the cross and Resurrection, we have no hope. There can be no self-help books when it comes to salvation. We ourselves are incapable of overcoming death. The fact that Jesus conquered death is the source of all of our hope. We have nothing to fear because nothing—not even death—can separate us from the greatest gift of all: the love of God in Christ Jesus. We have been sealed.

Scripture

For I am convinced that neither death, nor life, nor angels, nor principalities, nor present things, nor future things, nor powers, nor height, nor depth, nor any other creature will be able to separate us from the love of God in Christ Jesus our Lord. (ROMANS 8:38–39)

Prayer

Lord, God, help me to live without fear. Help me to look upon the Cross of Christ Jesus and to see that Jesus understands my greatest sufferings and my greatest fears, and that he has overcome them by conquering the greatest fear of all—death. Help me, Lord, to know, deep in my heart, that we shall overcome some day.

Chapter Six

Union Workers: The Church, Mary, the Saints, and Eternity

Construction workers face many dangers and hardships. For that reason, they seek strength in numbers by joining unions. Construction workers know that they are not lone rangers and that they have the support of their union when faced with difficult matters. It's always good to know that you are not alone. In matters of faith we do not stand alone, either. Through baptism, we have entered into union with Jesus and his Church.

A Union of Faith

The Lion's Club
The Boy Scouts of America
The Moose Lodge
The Country Club
A Fraternity or Sorority
The Royal Order of Water Buffaloes (from the Flintstones, remember?)

Lots of people belong to clubs. Clubs are wonderful. They bring people together. They often accomplish good things. We might think that belonging to the Church can be compared to belonging to a club.

Not really. We do not so much *belong* to the Church, as we *become* Church. The Church is not a club. A club is a loose association of like-minded people, gathered together for a specific purpose. As easily as you join a club, you can quit. The Church, on the other hand, is a living organism—the living Body of Christ—of which we are members, in the same way that hands, feet, arms, and legs are members of a body. As Catholics, we are no loose association of like-minded people. Through baptism, we are joined to one another in a profound and intimate way. We sometimes refer to people who are very close to one another as "joined at the hip." As members of the Body of Christ, we are joined to one another and to Christ at the heart, mind, and soul. We are in union with one another and with Christ.

Through baptism, we are joined to one another in a profound and intimate way.

Another way in which the Church is not a club is that a club is just one aspect among many in a person's life. In contrast, to belong to Church is to enter a community of faith whose members have committed every aspect—not just a segment—of their lives to Jesus. This is why we call Jesus "Lord." A lord is someone to whom you pledge allegiance and surrender control of your life. In baptism, we name Jesus as our Lord and turn our lives over to him.

"From the beginning, the Church was part of God's plan for sharing his divine life with all people."
(*USCC for Adults*, p. 113)

Try this activity—draw a pie chart of your life, dividing the pie into segments that show how much time you devote to the following aspects of life:

- **Work/school**
- **Sleep**
- **Family**
- **Play/recreation**
- **Exercise**
- **Rest**
- **Eating**
- **Spirituality**

Don't be surprised or disappointed if spirituality turns out to be the smallest slice of your pie. It's not because you aren't spiritual. It means that you need to expand your understanding of what it means to be spiritual. For many of us, we equate spirituality with those experiences that take place in church, at a church-related activity, or at prayer. With that as our criteria, our spirituality slice of pie will always be hopelessly small compared to the other slices.

In reality, our spiritual life is not a slice of the pie at all. It is the whole pie! We are not physical beings in search of a spiritual experience. We are spiritual beings having a physical experience in this life. Spirituality simply refers to our participation in the divine life. In baptism, you and I entered the Church through which we participate more deeply in the divine life. This means that everything we do is in communion with Jesus. Oh, of course we can and do choose to do certain things as if we were separate from him. At times we tell Jesus to "wait in the car" while we venture into various aspects of our lives that we prefer he not see. To be Church, however, is to recognize the omnipresence of God. It is to recognize and honor God everywhere and in everyone. Baptism does not make us members of an exclusive club. Rather, it makes us members of the living Body of Christ that is a sign to the whole world of the communion to which all people are called.

We are not physical beings in search of a spiritual experience. We are spiritual beings having a physical experience in this life.

Stewardship

To be Church is to practice stewardship, which is the sharing of our time, talent, and treasure with the faith community and beyond. Some of us wrongly conclude that in order to become more spiritual, we must spend more time in church and in church-related activities, even at the risk of interfering with our other relationships and responsibilities. The key to a deeper spirituality is not necessarily spending more time in church or in church-related activities. Although the Church does rely on people generously sharing their time, talent, and treasure, we do these things not to *become* more spiritual, but in response to the realization that we are blessed to share in the divine life. The key to being more spiritual is learning to recognize the presence of God in all things, in all people, and in all situations, and to respond by sharing our time, talent, and treasure with others.

Self-sacrificing Joe "Old Reliable" Febberman volunteers for one more committee.

Distinguishing Characteristics

We all have distinguishing characteristics: birthmarks, hair color, height, weight, and so on. The Church also has marks that reveal her identity. In fact, the Church's most distinguishing characteristics are called the *marks of the Church:* the Church is *one, holy, catholic,* and *apostolic.* Let's take a closer look at these four marks.

- **one**—the word *one* emphasizes the unity or oneness of Christ's Church, just as the Father, Son, and Holy Spirit are one. It means that within Christ's Church, there is both diversity and unity. We are held together as one by the Holy Spirit. Unfortunately, we humans have caused division within Christ's Church (such as the split between Roman Catholics and Eastern Orthodox, or the divisions that came about as a result of the Protestant Reformation). Through the efforts of *ecumenism* we seek to restore unity among all Christians. Our efforts to have better relationships with non-Christians are referred to as *interreligious dialogue.*
- **holy**—God alone is *holy.* This is simply a way of saying that God is God and we are not. To say that the Church is holy is to say that God is our source and our origin. As members of the Church, we are called to holiness, meaning that we are called to share in God's life and to reflect God-like qualities.
- **catholic**—There's *catholic* with a small *c* (meaning universal) and *Catholic* with a big *C* (referring to the Roman Catholic Church). When we say that we believe in one, holy, *catholic,* and apostolic church, we use a small *c.* We are saying that Christ's Church is universal. God calls all people to

The Church Is Not Man-Made

Although the Church is made up of humans, its origins and its guidance are divine. Jesus himself instituted the Church when he told his apostle, Simon, "[Y]ou are Peter, and upon this rock I will build my Church" (Matthew 16:18). Then, fifty days after his Resurrection and ten days after he ascended into heaven, Jesus sent his Holy Spirit upon the apostles on the Feast of Pentecost. We can think of Pentecost as the birthday of the Church. We are indeed human, but the Holy Spirit is with us, guiding the Church and inspiring us to carry out its divine mission.

salvation through his Church. Remember, the Church is not an exclusive club. It is a living sign of the unity to which God calls all people.

- **apostolic**—Jesus founded the Church upon Peter and then commissioned the apostles to go forth and baptize all nations. Since that time, the Church has remained faithful to the teachings of the apostles. We continue to be an apostolic church because the bishops, who are the successors of the apostles, safeguard, clarify, and proclaim the teachings of the apostles. The pope (the bishop of Rome) and the bishops are assisted by priests and deacons. Together, they gather and commission a vast army of the baptized to faithfully transmit the teachings of the apostles, as though passing along a priceless family heirloom, from generation to generation.

So when we say that "we believe in one, holy, catholic, and apostolic church," we are saying that we believe in a church that is unified in the Trinity, has divine origins and guidance, is open to all people, and is faithful to the teachings of the apostles. Those are some pretty identifiable marks.

Models of Faith—Mary and the Saints

Human beings, like all living creatures, learn through imitation. It is no surprise, then, that as we seek to grow spiritually, we look to others: parents, godparents, sponsors, and others who, by example, show us how to follow Jesus. The Church also gives us role models, the saints, who have faithfully followed Jesus by living lives of holiness. By learning about the lives of the saints, we can learn how to respond to God's call in our own lives.

Is There Salvation Outside of the Church?

What about Protestants, Muslims, Hindus, Jews, and a myriad of other non-Catholics? Can any of these people receive salvation if they are "outside" of the Catholic Church? The Church says that these people can indeed be saved. In the *Constitution on the Church in the Modern World #22*, the Church teaches that every human person is saved by Jesus Christ in ways known only to God. This means that we believe that the Catholic Church is the means of salvation, but that in ways known only to God, non-Catholics who seek God with a sincere heart and try to do his will as they understand it, are in a certain, though imperfect, communion with the Catholic Church, through which they can find salvation.

Among all of the Church's saints, the greatest example is Mary, the Mother of Jesus. Mary holds a special place of honor for Catholics. We do not worship her; but rather, we honor her. We do not pray *to* her; but rather, we pray *with* her and *through* her. Mary is the first and greatest disciple because she faithfully followed her own son, Jesus, even before he was born. She did so by saying "yes" to God's will, accepting her role as the mother of God's only Son. Because of Mary's role as the mother of Jesus, the Son of God, we honor her by calling her the Mother of God and the Mother of the Church. As our Mother, we can go to Mary for help, asking her to help us grow closer to her son, Jesus. By following Mary's example and through her intercession, we can become more faithful disciples of Jesus.

Big Words to Describe a Woman of Few Words

Except for her Magnificat in Luke 1:46–55, Scripture reveals Mary as a woman of few words (less than 200 total words are attributed to Mary in the Gospels and less than 50 when we subtract the Magnificat). However, we use some mighty big words when referring to some major events in her life that help us to understand her role in our salvation.

- **Immaculate Conception**: On December 8, we celebrate Mary's own conception (not the virginal conception of Jesus) free from original sin.
- **Presentation of Mary**: On November 21, we recall from a traditional story (not Scripture) that Joachim and Anne, Mary's parents, brought Mary to the temple to present her to the Lord when she was three years of age.
- **Annunciation**: On March 25, we recall the appearance of the Angel Gabriel, announcing to Mary that she is to be the mother of the Son of God (Luke 1:26–38).
- **Visitation**: On May 31, we recall the day that Mary, pregnant with Jesus, visited her cousin Elizabeth who was pregnant with John the Baptist (Luke 1:39–57).
- **Assumption**: On August 15, we celebrate Mary's being taken up to heaven, body and soul, after her death, where she enjoys the union of body and soul that we look forward to in the resurrection of the dead at the end of the world.

Mary is the greatest of all saints. The rest of them, however, aren't too shabby either! For centuries, people have looked to the lives of the saints for inspiration. In his book, *My Life with the Saints* (Loyola Press, Chicago, 2007), James Martin, SJ, explains why we do this:

> There's no reason to feel as if devotion to the saints somehow takes away from your devotion to Jesus: everything the saints say and do is centered on Christ and points us in his direction. In reading the lives of the saints, I also discovered that I could easily recognize myself, or at least parts of myself, in their stories. This was the aspect of their lives that I most appreciated: they had struggled with the same human foibles that everyone does. Knowing this, in turn, encouraged me to pray to them for help during particular times and for particular needs. (p. 7)

As with Mary, we honor the saints; we do not worship them. When we pray before statues or images of saints, we are seeking their intercession and inspiration to help us grow closer to Jesus. Statues, icons, medals, and other sacred images serve our senses, helping us to focus our prayer.

The Communion of Saints and the Afterlife

All of this talk about the saints leads us to address the next obvious question: what exactly do Catholics believe about the afterlife? After all, the saints are dead, aren't they? Well, yes and no. The fact is, we all die. However, Catholics believe that our souls are immortal. When we die, our souls and our bodies are separated. Depending on the extent to which we have either accepted or rejected God's love, our souls, reunited with our bodies at the Last Judgment, will spend eternity in heaven or hell.

- **Heaven** is that state of being in which we are in the presence of God—Father, Son, and Holy Spirit.
- **Hell** is that state of being in which we are completely separated from God. Hell is not imposed upon an individual externally by God, but is "chosen" by individuals who reject God's love and mercy.
- **Purgatory** is that state of transition and purification for those who die in the love of God, but who have not fully let go of that which separates them from that love. Before we enter into God's presence in heaven, we must be cleansed of every trace of sin. This cleansing is thought of as painful, in the same way that moving from a dark room into bright sunlight can hurt our eyes until they adjust. For this reason, we pray for those in purgatory to ease their transition.

Three buddies died in a car crash and they went to heaven for an orientation. St. Peter asked them, "When you are in your casket and friends and family are mourning you, what would you like to hear them say about you?" The first guy said, "I would like to hear them say that I was a great doctor and a great family man." The second guy said, "I would like to hear that I was a wonderful husband and school teacher, who made a huge difference in the lives of children." The last guy replied, "I would like to hear them say, 'Look! He's moving!'"

Because of our belief in the immortality of the soul, we Catholics believe that we can and do remain in communication with deceased faithful followers of Christ through the *Communion of Saints*. The Communion of Saints is made up of not only canonized (official) saints, but of all those faithful followers of Jesus who have passed from this life to the next: parents, grandparents, aunts, uncles, children, cousins, friends, neighbors, and so on. Through their prayers and intercession, we can be helped. By the same token, through our prayers, the souls in purgatory can find assistance. Like the cell phone company that assures its customers that they are backed by a network, we, too, are backed by a network of those who "have gone before us marked with the sign of faith." (Eucharistic Prayer I, *The Sacramentary*) We are not alone in this universe—and you don't have to believe in aliens to say that.

Only one thing can keep people from being afraid of the God of judgment: an encounter with Jesus Christ, God's "human face."
Benedict XVI

So What?

What difference does it make that Catholics believe in the *Church, Mary,* the *saints,* and the *afterlife*?

- **The Church**: It means that we do not gain eternal life as individuals, but as a people who, driven by confident hope, show selfless love to one another. The Church is the "vehicle" that carries us on the path to Jesus. Eternal life or salvation is not an individual goal but is a social reality. We are bound to one another.
- **Mary and the Saints**: It means that in them, we find role models who help us to live with confident hope. Mary and the saints are tried and true examples of how to follow Jesus. Since they are alive in the Communion of Saints, we can be in communication with them, seeking their assistance.
- **Heaven, Hell, Purgatory**: It means that we live in the present with confident hope because, in Jesus, we have been given a taste of eternal life—of "things to come." Our belief in eternal life is not just wishful thinking. In the risen Christ, we have "proof" of what awaits us if we follow in his way. We can live in certainty now—today—knowing that nothing can separate us from the love of Christ.

The Last Judgment

The idea of the Last Judgment—Judgment Day—strikes many of us as frightening. However, Pope Benedict XVI, in his encyclical *The Hope of Salvation* (*Spe Salvi*) wrote that "the last Judgment is not primarily an image of terror, but an image of hope" and that Christ himself is a "fire which both burns and saves." Catholics believe that immediately after death, each person comes before God for an individual (particular) judgment and experiences heaven, purgatory, or hell. The Final Judgment refers to the end of time, when Christ will return in glory and all will be raised from the dead to stand before God, at which time our relationship with him will be revealed to all. Jesus himself describes this last (general) judgment in Matthew 25:31-46. Pope Benedict XVI reminds us that only one thing can keep people from being afraid of the God of judgment: an encounter with Jesus Christ, God's "human face."

Scripture

Then I saw a new heaven and a new earth. The former heaven and the former earth had passed away, and the sea was no more. I also saw the holy city, a new Jerusalem, coming down out of heaven from God, prepared as a bride adorned for her husband. I heard a loud voice from the throne saying, "Behold, God's dwelling is with the human race. He will dwell with them and they will be his people and God himself will always be with them (as their God). He will wipe every tear from their eyes, and there shall be no more death or mourning, wailing or pain, (for) the old order has passed away." (REVELATION 21:1–4)

Prayer

Father, Son, and Holy Spirit, thank you for inviting me to share in your divine life as a member of your Church. Help me, loving Father, to learn from the example of Mary and the saints, to follow Jesus more closely, and to do your will with the help of the Holy Spirit. Lead me into a deeper, closer relationship with you now, so that having seen your face now, I will have nothing to fear at the time of Final Judgment.

PART TWO

The Sacraments: Expressing Faith

Chapter Seven

Using a Laser Level for Alignment: Worship and Liturgy

I desperately covet these new laser levels (also called laser straight edges) that allow you to perfectly align pictures, shelves, and anything else that needs to be lined up perfectly. I usually rely on my eyes to align things and, given the fact that I wear corrective lenses, that's probably not the best idea! In our spiritual lives, our quest is to be aligned with God. John the Baptist calls us to "Prepare the way of the Lord, make straight his paths" (Matthew 3:3). Our spiritual eyesight is often blurred. We need help making the proper alignment.

At a Loss—Hearing Loss, That Is

It so happens that I have a hearing problem. My right ear suffered some inexplicable nerve damage that resulted in significant hearing loss. Although I benefit from the use of hearing aids, I still need to physically either align myself with the person who is speaking or move closer so that I can comprehend what they are saying. On the one hand, it can be frustrating to always have to maneuver myself into position when someone is speaking. On the other hand, I have become a very attentive listener!

In a similar way, each of us, in a variety of subtle ways, is impaired and unable to clearly hear God's voice unless we align ourselves with him and move toward him. Our baptism—whether celebrated years ago in our infancy or more recently as an adult—is that experience in our lives which aligns us with God. To live our baptism each and every day of our lives means to strive to align

Our baptism is that experience in our lives that aligns us with God.

ourselves with God's will in all that we do, striving to turn and move toward him.

"I wanted to turn my life over to Christ and become a new person . . . someone more svelte"

In Hebrew, the word for *worship* (shachach) actually means "to bow before" in a posture of submission. To bow to someone or something is to physically orient ourselves or align ourselves with that person or thing. It is to say, in essence, "I direct all of my being—physical, emotional, and spiritual—to you." This is why the First Commandment directs us not to bow before any false gods. God is telling us that when we align ourselves with someone or something other than him, we are not aligned with our true source. No doubt this is why the very first words of Jesus' public ministry were, "Repent, and believe in the gospel" (Mark 1:15). To repent is to reform or to start over again. It means to die to our old self—to die to sin—and to be reformed, born anew, in the grace of God. No longer are we to be aligned with sin, but rather, we are to be aligned with the will of God.

As faithful Christians, we worship (align ourselves with) God, the Father of our Lord, Jesus Christ. We call our worship *liturgy,* which in Greek means "the work of the people" or "public work." In other words, liturgy is not something we do alone. It is something we do with or on behalf of the community of the faithful—the Church. Liturgy does not just refer to the celebration of the Mass, but to all of the official public prayers of the Church, such as the sacraments and the Liturgy of the Hours (more on that later). All liturgy, however, celebrates the Paschal Mystery of Christ. Through liturgy, the suffering, death, and resurrection of Jesus Christ become present to us and transform us. At the center of the Church's liturgical life are the sacraments, through which we move toward Christ and align ourselves with God.

The Sacraments of the Church

The *United States Catholic Catechism for Adults* reminds us that when a parent hugs a child, the hug is a visible reality, while the love that the hug conveys is an invisible reality. In a similar way, the sacraments are visible realities—outward signs—that convey for us the invisible reality of God's grace.

"When parents hug their children, for example, the visible reality we see is the hug. The invisible reality the hug conveys is love."
(*USCC for Adults*, p. 168)

Years ago, the *Baltimore Catechism* defined the *sacraments* as "outward signs instituted by Christ to give grace." Not a bad definition at all. The *Catechism of the Catholic Church* gave us another definition of the sacraments, which says much the same thing, but with more words: "The sacraments are efficacious signs of grace, instituted by Christ and entrusted to the Church, by which divine life is dispensed to us" (*Catechism of the Catholic Church,* 1131).

"When these sacramental signs are celebrated, they reveal and make present the reality they signify."
(*USCC for Adults*, p. 169)

WHAT DOES *EFFICACIOUS* MEAN?

We say that the sacraments are *efficacious* signs. Yikes! What does *efficacious* mean? Something is efficacious when it achieves an effect. For example, the words "I'm sorry" are efficacious–they achieve the effect of apologizing. So when we say that the sacraments are efficacious, it means that the signs, symbols, and rituals achieve the effect they represent. There's no magic involved. The signs, symbols, and rituals do not instigate God's action, but rather reveal and make present what God is doing in the lives of the people receiving that sacrament.

The seven sacraments of the Church can be grouped together in the following way:

- **Sacraments of Initiation**—Baptism, Confirmation, and Eucharist
- **Sacraments of Healing**—Penance and Reconciliation and Anointing of the Sick
- **Sacraments at the Service of Communion**—Holy Orders and Matrimony

Jesus himself instituted these sacraments and entrusted them to the Church. Through our celebration of the sacraments, we enter into the Paschal Mystery of Jesus (it's always about dying and rising . . . always!) and partake in the divine life of the Trinity. Through the sacraments, we worship God. We align ourselves with God and grow in holiness (God-likeness), both as individuals and as a community.

"A man can no more diminish God's glory by refusing to worship Him than a lunatic can put out the sun by scribbling the word 'darkness' on the walls of his cell."
C. S. Lewis

What Is the Liturgy of the Hours?

The Liturgy of the Hours, also known as the Divine Office or Daily Office, is the daily public prayer of the Church through which we praise God and make the entire day holy. It consists of readings in the middle of the night (Matins), a morning prayer of praise (Lauds), an evening prayer (Vespers), and night prayer (Compline). The psalms form the heart of the Liturgy of the Hours, all 150 prayed over three weeks. This liturgy also includes poetic texts from the Old and New Testaments, other Scripture readings, hymns, intercessions, and the Our Father. Priests, deacons, and many religious communities are committed to praying the Liturgy of the Hours each day. Lay people are also welcome and encouraged to do so.

The parish liturgy team met with the pastor to find ways to incorporate various worship styles in the parish. They decided on four different styles of celebrating the Mass. One Mass would be for those new to the faith. Another would be for those who preferred traditional worship. A third would be for those who had lost their faith and would like to get it back. The fourth Mass would be for those who had a bad experience with the Church and were complaining about it. To advertise the Masses, they suggested the following names for each: Finders, Keepers, Losers, Weepers. Thankfully, the pastor overruled!

Who? How? When? Where?

When it comes to understanding how we worship God through the sacraments, we need to ask four questions.

1. **Who celebrates the sacraments?** The Church, the entire Body of Christ, together with the Holy Spirit
2. **How do we celebrate?** We use many signs, symbols, and rituals. We read from Scripture. We walk in procession. We sing. We bow, kneel, stand, and sit. We gather in sacred space that speaks to us of the mystery of God. In short, we combine word and action to make visible the invisible grace of Christ. This action carries beyond the church walls, for we continue to worship God in our daily living by loving others selflessly, making grace visible through our actions.
3. **When do we celebrate?** Our celebration of liturgy throughout the year is centered on Sundays, the day on which we recall the resurrection of Jesus. The Liturgical Year, with Easter at its center, celebrates the Paschal Mystery of Jesus through various seasons and feasts. Throughout the liturgical year, we honor Mary and the saints, recalling how the Paschal Mystery of Jesus transformed their lives. The Liturgy of the Hours is the daily worship of the Church.
4. **Where do we celebrate?** Although we can and do pray anywhere and everywhere, the Church dedicates certain spaces as sacred. Church buildings provide us with dignified spaces that remind us of the significance of what takes place when we worship Almighty God—when we align ourselves with the Divine.

The Liturgical Year

The liturgical calendar represents the celebration of the mystery of Christ, from the anticipation of his birth; to his Incarnation; to his death, Resurrection, and Ascension; to the expectation of his return. The Church marks the passage of time with a cycle of seasons and feasts that invites us, year after year, to deepen our relationship with and commitment to Jesus.

The liturgical calendar represents the celebration of the mystery of Christ.

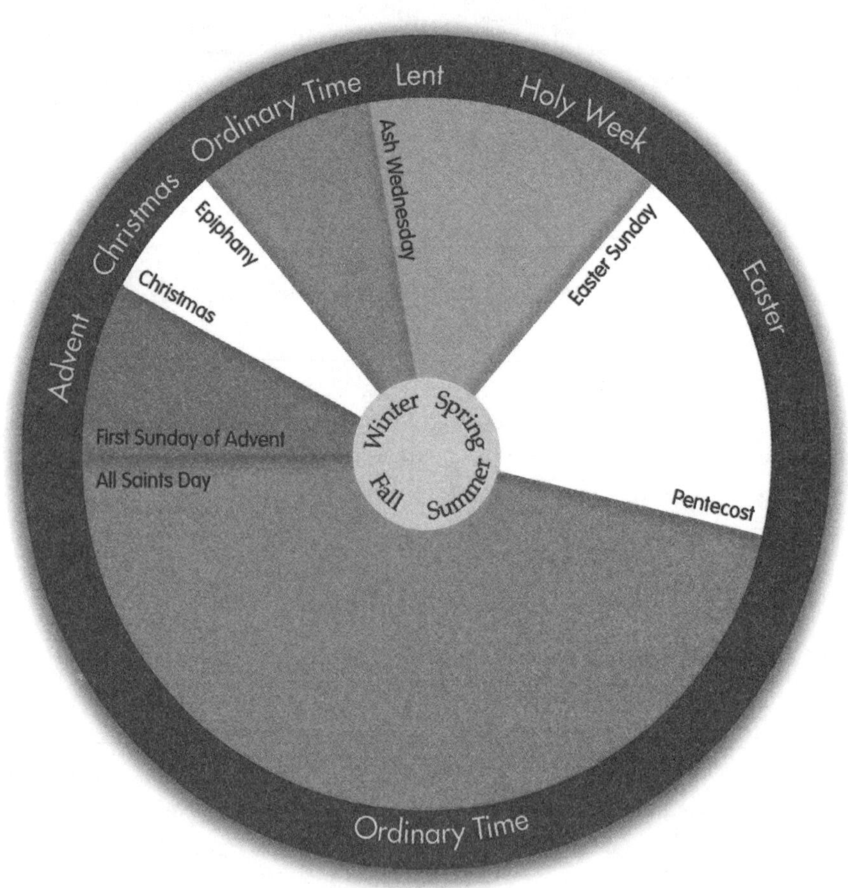

Advent marks the beginning of the Church year. It is a time of anticipation for Christmas, and it begins four Sundays before the Christmas feast. Advent is a season of hope and joyful anticipation in which we prepare to celebrate the birth of Jesus and anticipate his Second Coming.

The **Christmas** season includes the celebrations of Jesus' birth (Christmas) and his becoming known to the world (Epiphany). The Christmas season lasts until the feast of the baptism of the Lord.

Ordinary Time is the time set aside for celebrating our call to follow Jesus as his disciples day by day. Ordinary Time calls us to reflect upon the Paschal Mystery and our call to discipleship throughout the year. The Sundays of the entire year are counted (thus, ordinal or ordinary) or set aside as sacred time. Ordinary Time (typically 33 weeks) is celebrated following the Christmas season and then again following Easter.

Easter celebrates Jesus being raised from the dead. Because the Resurrection is the central mystery of the Christian faith, the Church sets aside fifty days of joyful celebration. These fifty days, from Easter to Pentecost, are celebrated as one feast day, sometimes called "the great Sunday." Easter is celebrated on the first Sunday after the first full moon of spring.

Lent, a season of conversion that begins on Ash Wednesday, is a time of turning toward God in preparation for Easter. It is not a somber or sad season, but one of sobering joy, for we know that the happiness of Easter will come. Throughout these forty days, the whole Church prepares by praying, fasting, and giving alms.

Holy Week is set aside for us to recall the events surrounding the suffering and death of Jesus, beginning with his triumphant entrance into Jerusalem on Palm Sunday and ending on Holy Saturday with the vigil of his Resurrection. We celebrate the culmination of the entire liturgical year by marking the Triduum (the "three days" of Holy Thursday, Good Friday, and Holy Saturday), our "Passover" celebration of Jesus' death and Resurrection.

Pentecost is the day on which we celebrate the coming of the Holy Spirit upon the disciples fifty days after Jesus' Resurrection. With this feast, the Easter season ends. Pentecost is our celebration of the "birthday of the universal Church."

So What?

What difference does it make that Catholics *worship*? It means that we continually strive to align ourselves with God's will. Without worship, we easily veer off path, often unknowingly sliding into patterns of life that take us away from loving God and neighbor, and instead keep us focused on ourselves. In a sense, we all suffer from a type of "spiritual amnesia." In other words, it is human nature to forget to pay attention to our spiritual dimension. Worship is our constant reminder that our lives need realignment, so as to be directed toward God who is love. In essence, to worship is to love, for to love is to direct all of our attention—our very being—to the presence of another.

Scripture

Then the devil took him up to a very high mountain, and showed him all the kingdoms of the world in their magnificence, and he said to him, "All these I shall give to you, if you will prostrate yourself and worship me." At this, Jesus said to him, "Get away, Satan! It is written: 'The Lord, your God, shall you worship and him alone shall you serve.'" Then the devil left him and, behold, angels came and ministered to him. (Matthew 4:8–11)

Prayer

Lord, God, I am so often tempted to direct my energies and attention to things other than you. Help me to align myself with your will, so as not to fool myself into thinking that anything other than you can bring me salvation. Help me to worship you; to direct my mind, heart, soul, and strength to you; so that I might not fall victim to spiritual amnesia, but will always remember that I was made to know, love, and serve you.

Chapter Eight

Construction Safety Signs: Mystery and Sacramentality

Construction sites are filled with safety signs that workers need to pay attention to: *High Voltage; Hard-Hat Area; Heavy Equipment Crossing; Overhead Crane; Restricted Area Authorized Personnel Only.* I know that if I were a construction worker, the most important sign for me would be: *Lunch Area!* Seriously, though, studies show that on-site safety promotion activities increases the extent to which workers recognize, comprehend, and pay attention to signs, lest they encounter danger. Catholic worship includes many signs which speak to us of the presence of God. We need to learn to recognize, comprehend, and pay attention to these signs.

It's a Mystery

Mystery novels are very popular. We love to be presented with a situation that temporarily mystifies us and challenges us to solve it before the sleuth in the story does. It's like putting a puzzle together: if we can locate all of the pieces and fit them together, we can get the whole picture and the mystery will be solved. In our culture, a mystery is something to be solved.

When we Catholics hear about the mystery of our faith, the Paschal Mystery of Jesus, the mystery of the Trinity, or the mysteries of the Rosary, we must wonder how we are supposed to solve all of these mysteries. We may even erroneously think that if we study theology, read the Bible, and master the thinking of the Fathers of the Church, we will be able to solve these mysteries and find fulfillment in life. In biblical tradition, however, a mystery is not something to be solved, but something to be entered into—to stand in awe of. In essence, a mystery is something that is revealed and yet remains hidden. Even though God has revealed himself to us throughout all of salvation history, culminating in the pinnacle of his revelation, Jesus Christ, God remains beyond our grasp. We can encounter God. We can know God. But we cannot solve God.

"You could read all of these books and none of them would really answer you but by the time you'd finish, you'd have learned to live with the question."

At Mass, just after the consecration, we are invited to "proclaim the mystery of faith." If a mystery is something that we simply can't understand, then the priest is inviting us to "proclaim what we don't understand!" The fact is, we cannot solve the mystery of faith and we may not fully understand it, but we can *know* it. In the deepest fiber of our being, we can and do know the mystery of our faith: Christ has died, Christ is risen, Christ will come again. This is the essence of the central mystery of our faith: the Paschal Mystery of Jesus. The word *paschal* comes from the Greek word for Passover, when the Hebrew people were saved by the blood of the lamb. We, in turn, are saved by the blood of the Lamb of God, Jesus, who is our Passover, our Pasch—thus, paschal mystery. The mystery at the heart of our faith is that from death comes new life. We may not fully understand this. We cannot solve this. But we know this in our heart of hearts that from death comes new life. Death is not the end.

A mystery is something that is revealed and yet remains hidden.

Learning a New Language—All Catholics Know Sign Language

I often ask Catholics if they know sign language and most respond by saying, "No." I then proceed to silently make the Sign of the Cross; to genuflect; to bow; to use my thumb to trace the cross on my forehead, lips, and chest; and to place my hands in the *orans position* (hands slightly extended with palms up). Folks quickly recognize what I am pointing out to them:

When it comes to expressing ourselves to God, words alone cannot do justice.

Catholics *do* know sign language. We are a sacramental people, expressing ourselves beyond words and relying on signs, symbols, and ritual gestures. Why do we bother? Because words alone are not enough, especially in relationships. When it comes to expressing ourselves to God, words alone cannot do justice. We engage our entire bodies in expressing ourselves to God, who himself speaks to us in ways that transcend words.

For Catholics, sacramentality is a language: the reliance upon signs, symbols, rituals, and gestures to express our encounters with God. Ultimately, sacramentality deals with the question *Where do you find God?* For some, God is a distant reality. Not so for Catholics. We believe that God can be found (is revealed) in all things, and yet remains a mystery. We do not equate the natural world with God (pantheism), nor do we believe that God is a distant reality (deism). Rather, we believe that the natural world is a reflection of God's transcendent presence and that all of God's creation is a channel of grace. We can call this way of seeing reality the Catholic sacramental sensibility.

"The world is charged with the grandeur of God!"
—Gerard Manley Hopkins, SJ

Because of our sacramental sensibility, it is no surprise that when we celebrate our encounters with God in the seven sacraments, we use ordinary things from the natural world—such as water, oil, fire, bread, and wine—as channels of God's grace. By the same token, in our prayers and devotions we are very comfortable using images and objects to assist us in our prayer. For Catholics, statues, holy cards, icons, rosaries, crucifixes, and other sacred images, which are referred to as *sacramentals,* draw our attention to God. We know full well that when we pray before a statue, we are not praying to or worshipping the statue. We certainly do not believe the statue is the manifestation of

"The Church celebrates the liturgy using an abundance of signs, symbols, and rituals."
(*USCC for Adults*, p. 171)

God, or Mary, or the saints. Rather, we use the images as reminders of God's grace and presence in this world.

The Catholic Church, then, is a sacramental faith. We worship beyond words, using sign, symbol, and ritual as God taught us. In contrast, many Protestant denominations are strictly word based. When the early Protestants reacted against abuses in the Church's sacramental system in the sixteenth century (sacraments were sometimes being sold), the Protestants proceeded to focus solely on the Word of God spoken in Scripture. As a result, more and more Protestant worship services abandoned any form of sacramental expression, turning to the spoken word. Many Catholics who occasionally have an opportunity to attend a Protestant worship service feel as though "something's missing." Even with excellent preaching, warm hospitality, and rousing hymn singing at a Protestant service, Catholics recognize that an entire portion of God's language is missing—sacramental language. God—who speaks through burning bushes, pillars of fire, columns of smoke, whispering breezes, and mighty winds—cannot be limited to spoken words. God—who instructed Abraham to ritualize the covenant (Genesis 15:8–21), who instructed Moses to remove his sandals in

A priest had been invited to give a mission talk about the Catholic use of signs and symbols in worship. As he was leaving the parish after his talk, he got into a serious car accident with a man who was a fallen-away Catholic, who had stopped at the church simply to warm up from the bitter cold outside. Both survived the accident unhurt and crawled out of the wreckage. The man recognized the priest as the presenter and said, "Father, I've been away from the Catholic faith for twenty years and stopped by the church tonight just to warm up. Our survival of this crash must be a sign from God that I am to return to the Church." The priest agreed it was, indeed, a sign from God. Then the man said, "Look, here's another sign from God. My car is completely demolished, but this bottle of wine didn't break. Surely God wants us to drink this wine and celebrate my return." So he handed the bottle to the priest, who took a few big swigs and handed the bottle back to the man. The man took the bottle, didn't drink at all, put the cap on, and handed it back to the priest. The priest asked, "Aren't you going to have any?" And the man replied, "No . . . I think I'll just wait for the police."

The Grinch Who Stole the Sacraments

In Dr. Seuss' story, *How the Grinch Stole Christmas,* the Grinch attempts to "steal" Christmas by pilfering all of its outward signs. To his dismay, the people in the village continue to celebrate Christmas despite the loss of these outward signs, because the inner reality could not be taken away. What if some Grinch tried to steal the outward signs of the sacraments—the water, oil, fire, bread, or wine? Would we Catholics still celebrate the inner reality of Christ's saving grace within? Of course! For us Catholics, the inner world and the outer world are intimately connected. To be sacramental is to see the presence of God reflected in the physical world. Catholics rely on the visible—signs, symbols, and gestures—to recognize and encounter the invisible God. The old *Baltimore Catechism* definition of a sacrament hit the nail on the head when it referred to sacraments as "outward signs."

the presence of the sacred (Exodus 3:5), and who gave the Israelites the Passover ritual (Exodus 12:1–20)—asks that we worship in his language, using sign, symbol, and ritual.

So What?

What difference does it make that Catholics worship using signs, symbols, and rituals? It means that when we worship, we use the very language that God uses; a language beyond words. This makes perfect sense since, at the very heart of our faith, is our belief in the Incarnation—that wonderful moment when the intangible became tangible. Jesus, then, is the sacrament of God, the language of God, the Word made flesh. If God speaks to all of creation in word and sacrament, and we are made in the image of God, then it follows that we, too, must speak God's language. Just as children learn to speak the words their parents teach them, we learn to speak the language of God, our Father in heaven.

Scripture

Then King Darius wrote to the nations and peoples of every language, wherever they dwell on the earth: "All peace to you! I decree that throughout my royal domain the God of Daniel is to be reverenced and feared: "For he is the living God, enduring forever; his kingdom shall not be destroyed, and his dominion shall be without end. He is a deliverer and savior, working signs and wonders in heaven and on earth, and he delivered Daniel from the lions' power." So Daniel fared well during the reign of Darius and the reign of Cyrus the Persian. (DANIEL 6:26–39)

Prayer

Lord, God, you have revealed your saving presence through signs and wonders. This is your language. Help me to open my eyes to the signs and wonders through which you continue to reveal yourself. Help me to enter more deeply into the signs, symbols, and rituals of the Church, so that I may hear your voice and recognize your presence in the celebration of the sacraments.

Chapter Nine

The Welding Process: Sacraments of Initiation

Welding is the process of joining metals by melting them and adding filler material to form a strong joint. I love watching welders in action. They look like astronauts, with their protective gear on and, once the sparks start flying, it becomes quite a spectacle. In the end, what you have is a bond that is forged. In the sacraments of initiation—Baptism, Confirmation, and Eucharist—a bond is forged between Jesus, the Church, and us.

I'm Melting!

In the movie *The Wizard of Oz,* the Wicked Witch of the West meets her doom when doused with water. It seems she melts when hydrated. As she slowly disintegrates, she cries out, "I'm melting! I'm melting!" Poor thing.

We normally associate the word *melting* with ice or candle wax. In both of these examples, a solid is transformed to liquid. In the case of wax, a candle can be reformed and reshaped. This image has long been applied to the human hart.

"My heart has become like wax, it melts away within me" (Psalm 22:15).

"The sacraments of initiation—Baptism, Confirmation, and the Eucharist—are the foundations of the Christian life."
(*USCC for Adults*, p. 183)

The image suggests that the human heart—thought of in the ancient world, as the center of one's emotions, thoughts, and knowledge—can be reformed and reshaped like wax. This reforming and reshaping of our lives is what we celebrate in the sacraments of initiation—Baptism, Confirmation, and the Eucharist. What we celebrate is not a once-and-done event, however. What we celebrate is the life-long dynamic of God inviting us to die to sin and our response of embracing his saving grace. Each day that we live in Christ, we are born anew. Our baptism is not an event of past memory. It is a renewable source of energy. It is a chronic condition from which we seek no cure. It is a bond that continues to be forged in the fire of the Holy Spirit each day of our lives.

Baptism

Reforming our lives is what baptism calls us to do. Baptism is the reason we celebrate the season of Lent (the forty days leading up to the celebration of new life in Jesus' Resurrection on Easter) each year. When adults make a decision to reform their lives, to turn away from sin, and to embrace Jesus in baptism, the Catholic Church walks with them on a journey of transformation called the *catechumenate,* also known as the RCIA (Rite of Christian Initiation for Adults). The *catechumenate* is a period of at least one year, during which time the catechumens—those preparing for baptism—learn to leave behind sinful ways and follow the Gospel message as taught by the Church. During the final forty days of their preparation for the sacraments of initiation, the entire church prepares with them, seeking to once again reform our lives by rejecting sin and embracing the grace of God in Jesus Christ.

Reforming our lives is what baptism calls us to do.

On Holy Saturday, at the Easter Vigil, the catechumens come forward to receive the sacraments of initiation. Although Baptism, Confirmation, and Eucharist are distinct sacraments, they are inseparable from one another.

⊕ **Baptism is our entrance, through death, into new life in Jesus' Church.**

"Well I don't think baptism off the high dive is a better symbol of commitment!"

- **Confirmation seals us with the gift of the Holy Spirit.**
- **The Eucharist completes our initiation, bringing us to the table of the Lord, where we eat the Bread of Life and drink from the Cup of Eternal Salvation.**

The dying and rising is complete. With our hearts melted and reformed by God's grace, we can say the words of Saint Paul, "yet I live, no longer I, but Christ lives in me" (Galatians 2:20).

The Liturgy of Baptism

The Rite of Baptism itself includes the following eight elements:

1. **The Sign of the Cross**
2. **Readings from Scripture**
3. **Exorcism and anointing**
4. **Blessing the baptismal water**
5. **Renunciation of sin and profession of faith**
6. **Baptism with water and the words, "I baptize you in the name of the Father, and of the Son, and of the Holy Spirit."**
7. **Anointing with sacred chrism**
8. **Reception of the white garment and the candle**

After the baptism of his baby brother, little Johnny sobbed in the back seat of the car all the way home. His father asked him three times what was wrong. Finally, the boy replied, "That priest said he wanted us brought up in a Christian home, but I want to stay with you guys."

Not YMCA but RCIA

The Rite of Christian Initiation for Adults (RCIA) is the normal procedure for preparing and welcoming new adults (and children of catechetical age) into the Catholic Church. The RCIA consists of the following stages:

1. **Inquiry**: A period during which people inquire about the Catholic faith and are introduced to the Gospels.

2. **Rite of Welcome**: In this liturgical rite, the candidates (now to be called catechumens) express a desire to respond to God's call and the Church accepts their expression.
3. **Catechumenate**: A period of formation and instruction, lasting anywhere from a year to two years, to foster conversion in the catechumen.
4. **Rite of Election**: A liturgical rite of election or enrollment of names, usually celebrated before the bishop on the First Sunday of Lent.
5. **Period of Purification and Enlightenment**: A period of forty days (Lent) of intense reflection on conversion and the upcoming reception of the sacraments.
6. **Sacraments of Initiation**: The celebration of the sacraments of initiation—baptism, confirmation, and Eucharist—during the Easter Vigil.
7. **Mystagogia**: A period of post-baptismal catechesis, known as mystagogy, in which the newly initiated enter more deeply into the life of the Church and reflection on the Paschal Mystery of Jesus.

What's Up with Infant Baptism and Limbo?

Infant baptism has a long tradition in the Church. Parents who want to give their children the greatest gift imaginable—salvation in Jesus Christ through the Church—commit themselves to bringing up the child in the Catholic faith, so that he or she may live out their baptism and embrace it fully as they mature. Often, parents felt compelled to baptize their infants immediately after birth to prevent them from spending an eternity in "limbo," should the infant die without receiving the saving waters of baptism. Limbo, thought of as a dull but somewhat pleasant state of being, despite being separated from the Beatific Vision, is not and never was an official teaching of the Church—but was rather a popular explanation for what happens to unbaptized children who die. Pope Benedict XVI has expressed his desire that the concept of limbo be relegated to history. Today, we confidently hope for the salvation of children who die without baptism, knowing that God wills that all people be saved.

Confirmation

In the movie *As Good As It Gets,* Jack Nicholson plays a character, Melvin Udall, who is a cranky and bigoted obsessive-compulsive, who finds a friend in a kind and patient waitress named Carol Connelly, played by Helen Hunt. Melvin is almost totally incapable of saying something nice until he finally musters up enough courage to pay the following compliment to Carol: "You make me want to be a better man." In this relationship, Melvin finds that he can benefit and grow as a person because of the gifts that Carol offers. Wanting to be a better man is the "fruit" of his relationship with Carol.

What Confirmation Is Not

Confirmation is not a Catholic bar mitzvah—some sort of a rite of passage from childhood into adulthood. Confirmation is a sacrament of initiation and can only be understood in relation to baptism and the Eucharist, the other two sacraments of initiation. Confirmation deepens our baptismal life and empowers us to go forth, strengthened by our relationship with the Holy Spirit, to participate in the mission of the Church.

We can benefit from any relationship when we are open to receiving what the other person offers. We can benefit from our relationship with the Holy Spirit by receiving what the Spirit offers us. So, how do we form a relationship with a dove?

Well, for starters the Holy Spirit is not a dove. Throughout Scripture, the Holy Spirit is described using metaphors: wind, breath, fire, a dove, just to name a few. While we're at it, the Holy Spirit is not an energy field, like "the Force" in Star Wars.

The Holy Spirit is one of the persons of the Trinity!

We speak of the Trinity as "three *persons* in one God," not, "two persons and a dove" or "two persons and a thing." This means that we can have a relationship with the Holy Spirit. Through baptism and confirmation, we do.

The Holy Spirit is one of the persons of the Trinity! We speak of the Trinity as "three *persons* in one God," not, "two persons and a dove" or "two persons and a thing."

The Gifts of the Holy Spirit

Through our relationship with the Holy Spirit, we benefit from seven gifts (based on Isaiah 11:2–3).

- **Wisdom**—the ability to recognize the importance of keeping God central in our lives
- **Understanding**—the ability to comprehend the meaning of God's message
- **Knowledge**—the ability to think about and explore God's revelation, and also to recognize there are mysteries of faith beyond us
- **Fortitude**—the courage to do what one knows is right
- **Counsel**—the ability to see the best way to follow God's plan when we have choices that relate to him
- **Piety**—the practice of praying to God in true devotion
- **Fear of the Lord**—an attitude of amazement before God, who is all-present, and whose friendship we do not want to lose.

In baptism, we receive the Holy Spirit, meaning that we enter into relationship with the Spirit. In confirmation, this relationship is sealed and strengthened. As a sacrament of initiation, confirmation is closely related to baptism. In practice, however, the two sacraments are often separated by many years. This happened when Christianity became the official religion of the Roman Empire in the fourth century and the numbers of people seeking initiation greatly increased. Unable to be present at every baptism, bishops granted permission to local pastors to preside over initiation and reserved the authority to later confirm those baptisms. This pattern has continued to the present day, resulting in a gradual distancing of confirmation from baptism and Eucharist.

The Second Vatican Council (1962–65) reaffirmed the unity of the sacraments of initiation through the restoration of the catechumenate (RCIA). At the Easter Vigil on Holy Saturday, local pastors are allowed to confirm newly baptized members of the Church who have participated in the RCIA.

How Do We Recognize the Holy Spirit

Do you believe in wind? Most likely, you do. Have you ever seen the wind? No. Wind is invisible. However, we can most certainly see its effects. In a similar way, we can recognize the presence of the Holy Spirit through the effects that the Spirit has on people. We call these effects the *Fruits of the Holy Spirit*. They are based on Galatians 5:22-23:

charity	joy	peace
patience	kindness	goodness
generosity	gentleness	faithfulness
modesty	self-control	chastity

The Liturgy of Confirmation

What are the visible signs that make present to us the invisible relationship we have with the Holy Spirit? Let's take a look:

- **Laying on of Hands**—The bishop extends his hands over those to be confirmed, calling on God for an outpouring of the Holy Spirit and the Gifts of the Spirit.
- **Anointing with Sacred Chrism**—The bishop anoints the forehead of those being confirmed and says the words, "Be sealed with the gift of the Holy Spirit."
- **The Bishop**—The bishop himself is an outward sign, representing the relationship that the Holy Spirit has with the entire Church, all the way back to the apostles.

Eucharist

I am always hungry. I can't help it. My metabolism is such that my stomach begins to growl pretty much every hour on the hour. I snack constantly to tame the tiger but within the hour . . . the growling returns.

Spiritually, I think most human beings are like that too. We are always hungry. We are always seeking something that will fulfill that hunger. In the Eucharist, we have the answer. God alone is our source of fulfillment. Nothing else! No one else! Not our looks, money, possessions, status, friends, family, geographical location, popularity, power, or abilities.

God alone.

That's what the Eucharist is all about. From the moment we enter the church building for Mass, we are being invited and challenged to realize that God alone sustains us. Challenged, because, throughout the rest of the week, we are being subtly seduced by a myriad of messages to believe that something else sustains us. Little by little, we can fall prey to those who tell us that we will find happiness if we buy certain clothes, drive a certain car, maintain a certain weight, have a certain body shape, live in a certain area or type of home, have a certain kind of job, make a certain salary, have a certain amount of sex, achieve a certain level of popularity, and wield a certain amount of power.

The message of the Eucharist is very clear: at our deepest level, we are incapable of sustaining ourselves. Every Sunday, when we receive communion, we are reminded that, although there's nothing inherently wrong with many of the things mentioned above, when we trust any of them to satisfy and sustain us, we have separated ourselves from our true source—the God who loves us.

The message of the Eucharist is very clear: at our deepest level, we are incapable of sustaining ourselves.

Source and Summit

When the Church teaches us that the Eucharist is the "source and summit" of our lives (*Catechism of the Catholic Church, 1324*), the Church is reminding us that God alone, who is present in the Eucharist, is our source of fulfillment. For Catholics, receiving communion is the ultimate acknowledgment that God is our source, is everything that we need.

When we come to recognize that God alone can satisfy our hunger and thirst, our lives find balance. In his book, *The Journey of Desire* (Thomas Nelson Publishers, 2000), author John Eldredge points out that we have three options: to be spiritually dead (desiring nothing, despairing), to be addicted (desiring the wrong things), or to be "alive and thirsty" (page 182). We come to recognize that this inner thirst, or, as Ronald Rolheiser refers to it, this *holy longing* (*The Holy Longing,* Doubleday, 1999), is ultimately a desire for God. This same recognition leads us to overcome the temptation to allow anything else to usurp God's role as the source of our satisfaction.

Living in a consumerist society, we may be tempted to treat the Eucharist as though it is a product and we are consumers. Naturally, like all consumers, we would expect immediate gratification. The Eucharist, however, is not a product. It's an embrace. Not a momentary embrace, but a lifelong one. Through our reception of the Eucharist, we are embraced by God, who heals and satisfies our inner ache.

At the same time, our reception of the Eucharist is an embrace, not only of God, but of our neighbors, as well. The Eucharist is not a "me and God" experience. To share a table is to enter into relationship with others. Likewise, we don't normally drink from the same cup that someone else is drinking from, unless we have an intimate relationship with that person. So we are, in a sense, becoming intimate with those who share the cup of communion. Our communion with God is thus fulfilled by loving our brothers and sisters. Communion compels us to recognize the presence of God not only in the bread and wine but also in the flesh of those we will encounter each and every day. Our worship of God, through the celebration of the Eucharist, is meaningless unless it points us in the direction of our neighbors.

"You wish to honor the body of the Savior? The same one who said: This is my body also said: You saw I was hungry and you didn't give me to eat. What you did not do to one of the least, you refused to me! So honor Christ by sharing your possessions with the poor."

(St. John Chrysostom, Homily 50 on Matthew)

The Mass

Catholics celebrate the Eucharist at Mass, the source and summit of our lives. As a ritual celebration, the Mass follows a particular pattern consisting of the following parts.

- **Introductory Rite**: The Mass begins with introductory rites that help us prepare to hear God's Word and to receive Jesus in Holy Communion.

  Opening Procession: The opening procession, led by our symbol of victory (the cross) and accompanied by joyful singing, represents our movement toward the altar of God.

  Penitential Rite: This rite includes a prayer of sorrow for sins and a petition for mercy (Lord Have Mercy, or Kyrie).

  Gloria: A hymn of praise, which is omitted during Advent and Lent.

  Opening Prayer: This prayer expresses our reason for coming together to celebrate and asks God for his grace.

- **The Liturgy of the Word**: We hear the story of God's plan for salvation, in the readings from the Old and New Testaments, arranged in a book called the Lectionary.

  First Reading: generally from the Old Testament

  Responsorial: from the Psalms

  Second Reading: generally from one of the New Testament Letters

  The Gospel: a proclamation of the Good News of Jesus from one of the four Gospels (Matthew, Mark, Luke, or John)

  Homily: the priest or deacon helps us understand our lives in relation to God's Word

  Profession of Faith: we express our faith and trust in God—Father, Son, and Holy Spirit, and in the Church

  General Intercessions: we confidently offer prayers for our needs and the needs of the world.

- **The Liturgy of the Eucharist**: We gather around the altar of sacrifice, to prepare to share in the sacred meal of the Eucharist.

  Preparation of the Gifts: A chalice (for the wine) and the paten (for the bread) are placed on the altar as the assembly practices stewardship through the collection. Members of the assembly carry bread and wine to the altar.

  Prayer over the Gifts: During this prayer, the priest prays that our sacrifice may be acceptable to God.

  Eucharistic Prayer: This prayer begins with the Preface—a song of praise to God—and the Holy, Holy (Sanctus), which is an Old Testament hymn of the angels. At the center of the Eucharistic Prayer is the consecration of bread and wine into the Body and Blood of Christ. The assembly proclaims, "Christ has died, Christ is risen, Christ will come again" (Memorial Acclamation). At the end of the Eucharistic Prayer, the priest holds up the host and chalice and sings a song of praise (a doxology) to the Trinity, to which the assembly responds with the Great Amen.

  Communion Rite: The Communion Rite consists of the Lord's Prayer, the Sign of Peace, the Breaking of Bread, the Lamb of God (*Agnus Dei*), and the reception of Holy Communion. After a brief period of

What Is the Real Presence of Jesus?

To the Hebrew mind, a living being was not thought of as a person within a body; the body and the person were seen as one and the same. In other words, when Jesus offers us his body, he is offering us his being, his very personhood. Likewise, in Jewish thought, blood was believed to be the source of life. This is why the consumption of meat containing blood was prohibited—life is strictly God's domain. When Jesus offers us his blood, he invites us to "consume" his very life. In essence, to receive the Eucharist is to consume the risen Christ and to be consumed into the Paschal Mystery of Christ. Our being and life come into communion with the risen Christ's being and life. The real presence of Jesus in the Eucharist means that we believe we are truly receiving the risen Christ's actual being and life, not just fondly recalling them. We refer to the transformation of bread and wine into the Body and Blood of Jesus Christ as *transubstantiation*.

silence to give thanks, the Communion Rite ends with the Prayer after Communion.

- **Concluding Rite**: The Concluding Rite consists of announcements, a blessing from the priest and a dismissal. It sends us forth on our mission as Christians.

So What?

What difference does it make that Catholics believe in and celebrate the sacraments of initiation—Baptism, Confirmation, and Eucharist? It means that we can be reformed. In celebrating the sacraments of initiation, we are reformed into followers of Jesus Christ. We are forged into union with Jesus and the Church. Through baptism, our sins are forgiven, and through confirmation, we are shown the way to the kingdom by the Holy Spirit. In the Eucharist—the real presence of Jesus in our lives—we find the nourishment that sustains us on this journey. The sacraments of initiation lay down for us the pattern of reforming our lives that we will follow the rest of our lives: dying to sin and, by the power of the Holy Spirit, rising to new life in Jesus Christ who sustains us. In the sacraments of initiation, our hearts melt like wax and are reformed and reshaped to conform to Jesus.

Where Does the Word *Mass* Come From?

In the Latin Mass, the priest or deacon dismisses the assembly with the words, "*Ite, Missa Est!,*" which means, literally, "Go, (the assembly) is dismissed!" The word *Mass* comes from this Latin word *missa,* which means *sent* or *dismissed.* The Mass, then, is the ritual celebration that sends us forth. For insight on just what we are being sent forth to do, see my book *Living the Mass: How One Hour a Week Can Change Your Life* (Loyola Press, coauthored with Fr. Dominic Grassi)

Scripture

Keep, then, this custom of the unleavened bread. Since it was on this very day that I brought your ranks out of the land of Egypt, you must celebrate this day throughout your generations as a perpetual institution.
(Exodus 12:17)

Prayer

Loving God, through Baptism you brought me out of slavery to sin and led me to freedom. Holy Spirit, in Confirmation, you guided me along the path, helping me to remain faithful. Lord, Jesus, Christ, you sustain me through the Eucharist, nourishing me so that I might continue the journey to the kingdom. Holy Trinity, thank you for the grace of the sacraments of initiation. May this grace which saves me from sin lead me to everlasting life. Amen.

Chapter Ten

Steamrollers: Sacraments of Healing

In the Chicago area, where I live, we talk about experiencing only two seasons: winter and road construction. The harsh Chicago winters result in numerous potholes that can cause a lot of damage. Of course, it's always a good sight to see a steamroller. It means that the repairs are nearing completion and the roads are being smoothed over. In our spiritual lives, the harsh realities of sin and sickness occasionally result in potholes that need repairs, lest they lead to further spiritual damage. Like a steamroller smoothing over freshly paved roads, the sacraments of healing—Reconciliation and Anointing of the Sick—smooth over the rough spots, paving the way for our journey to the Lord to continue.

In Need of Repairs

Some years ago, when my daughter was a teenager in high school, she got herself into a bit of a funk, feeling as though nothing was going right for her. After observing her sulking for a few days, I finally asked her what was going on that could make her so morose. She broke down in tears, citing a litany of woes. She then said something that caught my attention: "Why do bad things always happen to me? They never happen to any of my friends. Everything's always perfect for them, but things are always going wrong for me!" After I helped her to calm down and compose herself, I let her in on the big secret of life: "Everybody is broken," I told her. "Some people hide it better than others but deep down, everybody is broken and needs to be fixed. The sooner you accept that fact and realize that God alone can fix you, the healthier you'll be."

Along with my daughter, all of us feel at one point or another like poor Job, wondering what we might have done to deserve the various hardships that have come our way. We can respond in different ways.

- **We can grow envious of others who seem to have it easier than us.**
- **We can grow bitter and lash out at God for saddling us with undeserved burdens.**
- **We can fall into the pit of despair.**
- **Or, we can do what St. Paul taught us to do: recognize the strength and power of God in the midst of our weakness.**

In other words, we can embrace the fact that we are essentially broken and that our true strength comes from one source: God alone. In the realization that God's grace alone sustains us, we find healing.

In the realization that God's grace alone sustains us, we find healing.

I've Fallen and I Can't Get Up

Some years ago, there was a television commercial that portrayed an elderly person in need of assistance, lamenting, "I've fallen and I can't get up." Although this phrase became part of pop culture and was often made light of, the spirit of these words is truly at the very heart of Catholic spirituality. It is this realization—that at our deepest core, we are unable to sustain ourselves—that opens us up to the healing grace of God that comes to us through Jesus Christ. Christianity is not about picking ourselves up by our bootstraps when we've fallen. It is about first admitting that we have fallen and then turning to the One, and the only One, who lifts us up and sustains us. Does this mean that we sit idly by and allow God to do

"Through the gifts of the Church, Jesus, our divine physician, has given us the Sacraments of Healing—Penance and Reconciliation and Anointing of the Sick—for the forgiveness of sins and the ministry to the sick and the dying."

(*USCC for Adults*, p. 235)

all the work? No. But it does mean a clear recognition of and appreciation for whose hand it is that is reaching out to pick us up.

The essence of Christianity is salvation in Jesus Christ, who saves us from sin and death. Nothing brings us closer to the realities of sin and death than physical and spiritual sickness. When our lives are marred by the darkness of sin or the despair of physical illness, we come face to face with the realization that we are broken and in need of healing. It is at these times that Jesus comes to us in the sacraments of healing—Reconciliation and the Anointing of the Sick.

The Sacrament of Penance and Reconciliation

With increased emphasis on self-esteem education in recent years, and as a result of the "I'm OK, you're OK" pop psychology of recent decades, the notions of sin and brokenness have been all but lost. This is unfortunate. Don't get me wrong. It is very important for us to feel good about ourselves. There is a fine line, however, between healthy self-esteem and unhealthy self-righteousness. Self-esteem is embracing who we are with all of our faults and limitations. Self-righteousness is believing that we have no need for improvement. I am not suggesting that we need to wallow in our sinfulness and return to the days of instilling guilt and fear as the primary motivators of a spiritual life. Without a sense of sin and brokenness, however, we have no need for salvation. If we are to claim Jesus as our Savior, needing to be saved from something is a prerequisite!

Jesus made it quite clear that he came to save us from sin, and he was most critical of those he accused of being self-righteous (Matthew 23:28). The Gospels reveal, time and time again, Jesus showing mercy and forgiving sin. Even as he was dying on the cross, Jesus uttered words of forgiveness: "Father, forgive them, they know not what they do" (Luke 23:34). Mercy cannot be accepted by the self-righteous, but only by those who recognize their dependency—which is why only those who can become like children will enter the kingdom of heaven. It is Jesus' forgiveness that we embrace in baptism when we die to sin and rise again to new life in him. Baptism, however, is not the end of our conversion experience but is the beginning of ongoing conversion in Jesus Christ. When we sin, which we unfortunately continue to do even after Baptism, we are invited to renew our baptism through the Sacrament of Penance and Reconciliation, and to experience anew God's mercy.

But Why Do I Need to Confess My Sins to a Priest?

"So why do I need to go to a priest to have my sins forgiven?" This is the question that gets to the heart of the Catholic understanding of forgiveness. It is also a question that many Protestants ask of Catholics. The answer is really quite simple. First, we Catholics believe that Jesus forgave sin once and for all from the cross, and that, in baptism, we have found salvation and forgiveness of sins. When we sin, we can and should go to our room and ask the Lord for forgiveness. At this point, however, Catholics take it further. Remember, we are a sacramental church, meaning that we express outwardly and tangibly what is happening in the intangible world of our spiritual lives. The acts of going to a priest, verbally naming the sin—making it tangible—and hearing the words of forgiveness spoken by the priest ("I absolve you in the name of the Father, and of the Son, and of the Holy Spirit") are outward signs of the inner world of sin and forgiveness.

A Sacrament by Any Other Name Is Still a Sacrament

So, what's with all of the names for the sacrament in which Jesus forgives sins?

- Reconciliation
- Penance
- Penance and Reconciliation
- Confession

These all refer to the same experience of receiving forgiveness of our sins by Jesus through confession to a priest. The *Catechism of the Catholic Church* refers to this sacrament as the sacrament of penance and reconciliation (*Catechism of the Catholic Church,* 1440).

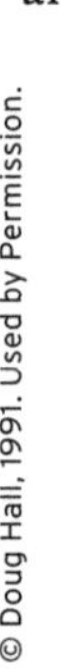

"I'm sorry for what I've done . . . even though some people think my little imperfections make me more endearing."

Think of it this way. If someone you are in love with never says the words "I love you," then that love suffers. The words "I love you" are efficacious when spoken by people who are truly committed to one another. They achieve the effect that they express. The same is true for the words, "I'm sorry" and "I forgive you." If someone you are in love with cannot say the words "I'm sorry" or "I forgive you," then the relationship suffers. These words are also efficacious. Saying the words "I'm sorry" or "I forgive you" actually complete the experience of reconciling a relationship. All of this applies to our Catholic understanding of forgiveness in the Sacrament of Penance and Reconciliation. Unless we can name our sins and say the words "I'm sorry," and hear the words of Jesus actually spoken—"I forgive you"—then our relationship with Jesus and others suffers. The Sacrament of Penance and Reconciliation, like all sacraments, is efficacious: it achieves that which it expresses.

The Seal of Confession

In the Sacrament of Penance and Reconciliation, the dignity of the person is of the greatest importance. The priest is bound to absolute secrecy regarding the sins confessed to him. This secrecy is called the "sacramental seal" (*Catechism of the Catholic Church*, 1467).

Naming the Sin

The wisdom of "naming the sin" can be found in one of the most healing experiences of our day, the twelve-step approach to overcoming addictions. The founders of this approach recognized that unless the sin—the addiction—is named and revealed to at least one other human being, the healing cannot truly begin. Without naming the sin or the addiction and sharing it with another human being, the individual runs the risk of living in denial, which prevents true healing from beginning.

In Europe, an old man was feeling guilty about something he had done, so he decided to go to confession. He said, "Bless me, Father, for I have sinned. I feel terrible because, during World War II, I hid a refugee in my attic." The priest said, "But that's not a sin! I wouldn't feel bad about that if I were you!" "But," the man replied, "I made him agree to pay half of my rent as long as he stayed." The priest said, "Well, I admit that certainly wasn't the noblest thing to do, charging the man to save his life. But you did save his life, after all, and that is a good thing. Don't worry about it too much; God forgives." The man said, "Oh thank you, Father. That eases my mind. I have only one more question to ask you: do I have to tell him the war is over?"

All of this leads to an interesting point. Over the last few decades, the number of people going to confession has dramatically decreased. During that same time period, however, the number of people naming their sins in twelve-step programs or entering therapy has dramatically increased. The bottom line is that people need healing. We need to reclaim the profound wisdom inherent in the Sacrament of Penance and Reconciliation and help people to recognize the great benefits of talking about our sinfulness with another human being—the priest—and hearing the words of forgiveness actually spoken out loud in a human voice.

The Liturgy of Reconciliation

Ordinarily, the sacrament of penance and reconciliation includes the following elements:

- **greeting and blessing from the priest**
- **a reading from Scripture (optional)**
- **confession of sins by the penitent**
- **the giving and accepting of a penance**
- **an Act of Contrition**
- **the priest's absolution**
- **a proclamation of praise by the penitent**
- **dismissal of the penitent by the priest**

"Here bring your wounded hearts, here tell your anguish; Earth has no sorrow that Heaven cannot heal."
—St. Thomas More

The Four "-tions" of reconciliation

The sacrament of penance and reconciliation includes the following:

- **Contrition**—We identify our sins through an examination of conscience, express sincere sorrow for our sins, and commit ourselves to not repeating them.
- **Confession**—We name the sins aloud to the priest.
- **Absolution**—We are set free (loosened) from our sins by the priest through the words of absolution.
- **Satisfaction**—We strive to repair the damage our sins have caused by performing works of penance.

The Anointing of the Sick

Tom Cruise doesn't get it. You may recall a few years ago that the actor publicly chided fellow actor Brooke Shields for taking antidepressants to combat postpartum depression. Cruise, an adherent of Scientology, claimed that if Shields and others suffering from depression would just think right and take some good vitamins, they would be fine. While it is true that science and medicine sometimes focus solely on the physical and ignore the emotional/spiritual, some religions or philosophies focus solely on the emotional/spiritual at the expense of the physical. Cruise's insistence that people should refuse medical treatment for depression is similar to the refusal of blood transfusions and other medical treatments by some Christians who claim that prayer alone is the answer. The truth is, the emotional, spiritual, and physical are intimately interwoven and must be treated as such. Catholics do not refuse medical treatment in favor of prayer. We seek the assistance of science and medicine while, all along, praying and trusting in the healing grace of Jesus Christ. We don't choose between healing of the body or healing of the soul. We seek both because they are inseparable.

Physical illness brings us face to face with our mortality, our fragility, and our vulnerability.

Since Jesus, without losing his divinity, became fully human, he understood the interwoven nature of the physical, emotional, and spiritual realities of humanity. Jesus prefaced many of his physical healings with the words, "Your sins are forgiven"—strange words if spoken by someone strictly concerned with the physical realm. Jesus healed people, not simply out of a passion for physical wellness, but to draw attention to the much deeper healing needed at the spiritual level. The healings that Jesus performed were powerful signs of the presence of the Kingdom of God in our midst. Through the sacrament of the anointing of the sick, we celebrate the Kingdom of God in our midst: a kingdom of healing, compassion, and mercy.

There's a very good reason that human beings visit, send cards and flowers, and otherwise pay attention to other human beings who are in the hospital because of physical illnesses. We know that their physical illness has emotional and spiritual implications. Physical illness brings us face to face with our mortality, our fragility, and our vulnerability. In other words, it makes us afraid. Fear is the opposite of faith. When we are filled with fear, we are unable to trust. And when we are unable to trust, we are unable to hope. And without hope, we are unable to love.

What better time to encounter Jesus?

The Sacrament of the Anointing of the Sick, like all of the sacraments, is an encounter with the living Christ. It is an encounter with Jesus when we need him most: when we are on the threshold of faith or despair, trust or fear. The Sacrament of the Anointing of the Sick is a sacrament of healing. There's no magic involved. Just as illness affects us at the physical, spiritual, and emotional levels, so, too, does healing. Encountering Jesus, who is compassionate and merciful, lifts our hearts and fills us with confidence, trust, and hope. This spiritual healing can, and often does, bring about healing on the physical level as well. Through the anointing of the sick, we come to the realization that with Jesus in our midst, we have nothing to fear because even death cannot separate us from his love.

Who Is the Sacrament of Anointing of the Sick For?

Anointing of the sick is not needed for someone who has the common cold. Although one may feel miserable from sniffling, sneezing, coughing, aching, fever, and not sleeping, the common cold does not typically bring us face to face with our mortality. On the other hand, the anointing of the sick is not reserved solely for those who are at death's door. So who is it for? Simply put, it is for anyone suffering from a *serious* illness or condition. The word *serious* gives us direction without placing severe restrictions on the celebration of the sacrament. The rite calls for a "prudent or reasonably sure judgment, without scruple." (*The Rites of the Catholic Church,* Pastoral Care of the Sick, General Introduction, 8). In general, this means that those to be anointed may include

- **those preparing for surgery**
- **those who suffer the weakness of old age**
- **children who are seriously ill**
- **those with chronic illness or addictions**
- **those suffering from serious mental health problems**
- **anyone else whose health is seriously impaired by sickness**

Likewise, the sacrament may be repeated if the sick person recovers after being anointed and becomes ill again, or if during the illness the person's condition worsens.

The Liturgy of Anointing of the Sick

Years ago, the anointing of the sick was considered a private matter between the priest and the sick person. Today, however, the Church emphasizes the communal nature of the sacrament and encourages family and friends to be present for the ritual, which includes the following:

- **a penitential rite**
- **Liturgy of the Word**
- **laying on of hands: the priest lays his hands on the head of the sick person**
- **anointing with the Oil of the Sick: the priest anoints the forehead and hands of the sick person and says, "Through this holy anointing may the Lord in his love and mercy help you with the grace of the Holy Spirit. May the Lord who frees you from sin save you and raise you up" (*Catechism of the Catholic Church,* 1513)**
- **Viaticum: for those who are near death, the priest offers the sacrament of penance and reconciliation and the Eucharist—*Viaticum* means food for the journey**

So What?

So what difference does it make that Catholics celebrate the Sacraments of Reconciliation and the Anointing of the Sick? It means that we encounter God in our brokenness. Our world despises brokenness and, indeed, brokenness is not something to relish. Our faith, however, teaches us that it is in our brokenness that we are most capable of recognizing the presence of God in our midst. This is why we keep crucifixes in our homes. We look to a symbol of brokenness to represent our salvation. It was through Jesus' brokenness and his Resurrection that we are saved. When we are broken by sin or by the burden of serious illness, we turn to God in all of our vulnerability for healing. The sacraments of healing smooth over the spiritual potholes that prevent us from journeying to the Lord.

Scripture

The Pharisees and their scribes complained to his disciples, saying, "Why do you eat and drink with tax collectors and sinners?" Jesus said to them in reply, "Those who are healthy do not need a physician, but the sick do. I have not come to call the righteous to repentance but sinners."
(LUKE 5:30–32)

Prayer

Lord, Jesus, you are my Divine Physician, the healer of my soul, my body, and my spirit. I pray that I may turn to you in my brokenness, knowing that through your death and Resurrection, you have overcome all evil, even death. Heal me of my sinfulness and fill me with your grace. In my times of illness, stretch forth your healing hand and restore me to health. I pray for all those who are sick and suffering. Lord, may they experience your healing compassion. Amen.

Chapter Eleven
Installing New Windows: Sacraments at the Service of Communion

A few years ago, my wife and I decided to have new windows installed in our home. What's interesting about windows is that, for the most part, you don't notice them. Oh sure, the frames may attract attention, but the main part of the window—the glass—is transparent. Ultimately, the purpose of a window is to not draw attention to itself, but to that which lies beyond it. As followers of Jesus, we are not supposed to draw attention to ourselves, but to the presence of the risen Christ in our midst. The Sacraments at the Service of Communion—Matrimony and Holy Orders—uphold two vocations in which people are called to be transparent, not drawing attention to themselves but to the needs of others.

It's Not about You

Babies are born into this world completely self-centered, incapable of caring about anything other than their own needs. When babies are hungry, tired, wet, or otherwise burdened, they cry for attention, demanding that their needs be tended to. Perhaps, then, the cruelest and yet the most necessary lesson in life is learning that "it's not about you." Indeed, this is the single most distinguishing quality between a child and an adult—the ability to put aside one's own needs and to put the needs of others first. This is not easy to do

Indeed, this is the single most distinguishing quality between a child and an adult—the ability to put aside one's own needs and to put the needs of another first.

when society encourages us to put ourselves first, to take care of ourselves, to think about ourselves, to pamper ourselves, and to think highly of ourselves. While there's nothing wrong with a healthy self-esteem, the fact is, excessive focus on one's self is actually contrary to the gospel. Jesus put it very bluntly when he said, "Whoever wishes to come after me must deny himself, take up his cross, and follow me" (Matthew 16:24).

The Catholic faith challenges us to live in such a way that we place the needs of others before our own needs. Beginning with Baptism, we commit ourselves to live as members of the Body of Christ. We recognize that Jesus is the vine and we are branches. We are not lone rangers. We are not free agents. We are at the service of the community.

Holy Orders and Matrimony belong to the Sacraments at the Service of Communion. This means they are primarily directed toward the salvation of others.

(*USCC for Adults*, pp. 262–63)

This commitment to the service of the community is further signified by the Sacraments of Matrimony and Holy Orders. These vocations reveal to us the selfless love that all of the baptized are called to share. For this reason, the Sacraments of Matrimony and Holy Orders are referred to as the Sacraments at the Service of Communion.

The Sacrament of Holy Orders

Throughout all of human history, priests have been seen as mediators between the human and the divine. We can call Jesus our "high priest" because he is the perfect and ultimate mediator between heaven and earth. In Jesus' Incarnation, humanity and divinity are joined. Through Baptism, we all share in the priesthood of Jesus, and we are no longer separated from God. We call this the *common priesthood.* To build up this common priesthood, the Church provides us with an ordained priesthood—bishops, priest, and deacons. The ordained priesthood is not another level

The ordained priesthood is not another level of priesthood inserted between us and God, but rather it serves to maintain the health of the common priesthood and serves as a sign of the intimate connection with Jesus that all of the baptized share through Baptism.

But I Thought They Were Perfect!

As an eighth-grade catechist, I once accompanied my students to church for a communal celebration of the Sacrament of Reconciliation. After all of the students had gone to confession, I noticed one of the priests walk over to a fellow priest to confess to him. I drew the attention of some of my students and quietly said, "See, priests go to confession too." One of the young people observed this and said, "But I thought they were perfect!" I explained that priests are like all of us—called to be holy, but possessing human frailty. Priests are not perfect. They are, however, ordained to live as outward signs of holiness, so there is greater scrutiny of their behavior. By virtue of our common baptism, however, we are all—priests and lay people alike—called to live lives of holiness.

of priesthood inserted between us and God, but rather it serves to maintain the health of the common priesthood and serves as a sign of the intimate connection with Jesus that all of the baptized share through Baptism. Like a window, the priesthood is not intended to draw attention to itself, but is to be transparent, drawing attention only to Christ.

The Sacrament of Holy Orders consists of three kinds of participation

- **Bishops**—A bishop receives the fullness of the Sacrament of Holy Orders and is the head of a local church or diocese. He is also part of the episcopal college, which refers to the bishops of the world together with the pope. Bishops may administer all of the sacraments. Only bishops may ordain priests. Ordinarily, confirmation is reserved for the bishop unless he delegates that authority to pastors, such as on Holy Saturday, when priests may confirm at the Easter Vigil.
- **Priests**—A priest serves the community in a variety of ways, such as presiding at liturgies, preaching, administering the sacraments, counseling, serving as pastors of parishes, and teaching.

"We're here to install the new pastor. Where do you want him?"

A young, newly ordained priest noticed, after a few weeks at his first parish, that people were falling asleep during his homilies. Dismayed, he sought out the pastor. "Father, people are falling asleep during my homilies. What can I do?" "Well, my boy," answered the pastor, "it's all a matter of practice. For the next week, sit in your study and practice your homily in front of a mirror, adding some gestures and varying your voice tone." Encouraged, the young priest did as the pastor had suggested. Come Friday, the two priests were having lunch. The pastor asked, "Well, how did it go?" "I'm not sure," replied the young priest. "I fell asleep."

- **Deacons**—A deacon assists the bishop by serving the needs of the community, proclaiming the Gospel, teaching and preaching, baptizing, witnessing marriages, and assisting the priest at liturgies. Some deacons are transitional, meaning that they are preparing to serve as priests, while other deacons are called to remain deacons for life and to serve the Church in this capacity. These deacons may be married.

The Liturgy of Ordination

The rites of ordination for bishops, priests, and deacons consist of the following essential elements:

- **The imposition of hands**—The bishop imposes his hands on the head of those being ordained.
- **The words of consecration**—The bishop asks God to pour forth the Holy Spirit and his gifts upon those being ordained.

What's Diocesan and What's Religious?

Don't all priests take vows of poverty, chastity, and obedience? Actually, no. Only priests who belong to religious communities (such as the Jesuits, Franciscans, Dominicans, etc.) take these vows. For religious, poverty means to have no personal ownership of things, but rather to share them as a group; chastity means to live a life of celibacy; and obedience means to be accountable to the superior and to the community. Typically, parish priests are diocesan priests who serve the local bishop. Diocesan priests make a promise of celibacy and promise obedience to their bishop. They are not bound to a life of poverty. However, like all the baptized, they are called to live a life detached from material goods.

- **Anointing with oil**—Bishops are anointed with oil that is poured on their heads, while priests are anointed with oil on their hands.

Matrimony

Matrimony is another sign of the call of all the baptized to be concerned with the salvation of others. The selfless love of a man and a woman in a lifelong commitment to one another, and to the children they bring forth into the world, is a living sign of the selfless and life-giving love that God has for us. It is also a living reminder to all who are baptized that we are all called to share this selfless love with one another.

For most of the sacraments, bishops, priests, and deacons administer the rite. Of course, in danger of death, anyone can baptize. But what about marriage? Who administers this sacrament? Actually, the man and woman entering into the marriage confer the sacrament upon each other by expressing their consent in the presence of a minister of the Church, two witnesses, and the congregation. And just what is this consent? It is consent to give oneself fully to one's spouse, expressed in its deepest form through the consummation of the marriage. Thus, it is no stretch of the imagination to say that, for Catholics, sexual intercourse between a married man and a married woman is sacramental. This outward sign of love and fidelity shared privately forms the couple into a living and public outward sign of God's love and fidelity. There is no higher expression of love than the total self-giving of one person to another. When two married people selflessly offer themselves, body and soul, to one another in sexual intercourse, they are joining in the celebration of God's selfless love for all mankind. It is for these reasons that this precious form of expressing love is to be reserved for marriage.

Too often, the Church is seen as having a negative attitude about sex. The truth is, because we believe that sexual union is sacred, we safeguard it. Like a priceless painting on display in an art gallery, we protect against any casual behaviors that might harm it. What we need to do as a Church is to boldly preach that the sexual encounter between a husband and wife is sacramental. Just as we encourage frequent reception of the Eucharist as a means of encountering Jesus, we should be encouraging married couples to encounter God's grace frequently through sexual expression. We need to invite people to recognize the beauty and sacredness of married sexual expression, and then explain that we safeguard sex because it is sacramental.

We can't just stand against sex outside of marriage. We need to stand *for* sex within marriage.

"Ah, Jerry . . . they're playing our song."

God's Fidelity

Marriage has long been seen as a symbol of God's love and fidelity for his people. The Old Testament contains many references to God's relationship with his people as a marriage. Perhaps the most powerful of these is found in the Book of Hosea. The prophet Hosea was married to an unfaithful wife, Gomer. Despite her infidelity, Hosea took her back. Gomer symbolized the infidelity of God's people. Just as Hosea would not give up on his unfaithful wife, God cannot, does not, and will not renounce his people, his betrothed. For this reason, the marriage covenant is seen as symbolic of the covenant that God has made with his people—a covenant that continues today through Jesus and the Church.

Poverty, Chastity, and Obedience in a Marriage

When I was teaching religion in a high school seminary, we discussed the concepts of poverty, chastity, and obedience in religious life. One of my students said, "That sounds too difficult. I'd rather get married." Boy, did he open the door for a discussion! As a married man, I told him that married people are called to practice these virtues as well.

- **Married people practice a spirit of poverty by sharing all things in common with the family. Paychecks that used to go into a private bank account are now often spent on family needs before the check is even deposited.**

Unitive and Procreative

Catholic marriages are both *unitive* and *procreative*. *Unitive* means that the couple is solemnly bonded one to the other. *Procreative* means that the consummation of the marriage leads to the gift of life—the birth of children. For Catholics, this is not an either/or situation. It is both.

- **Married people practice chastity. Like all the baptized—married, single, or celibate—married people are sexual beings, called to relate to others in the appropriate manner. Married people are celibate to everyone in the entire world except for one person—their spouse.**
- **Married people are called to practice obedience. This does not mean that one spouse says, "Jump" and the other replies, "How high?" It means that married people are accountable to one another and to their children. Married couples have voluntarily sacrificed their individualism to live in community—their family, which is the domestic church.**

Religious priests, brothers, and sisters who live these solemn vows, are signs to all of the baptized of what we are called to practice as disciples of Jesus.

Divorce, Communion, Annulments

For some people, for a variety of reasons, divorce is the only possible recourse. Divorced Catholics often wrongly assume they can no longer receive Holy Communion. This is only true when divorced Catholics have remarried without an annulment of their first marriage. An annulment is not a Catholic divorce. It does not mean that a marital relationship did not exist, nor does it mean that the children of that marriage are illegitimate. It means that there was no sacramental bond. Once an annulment has been granted, divorced Catholics are free to have a sacramental marriage.

The Liturgy of Marriage

The essential element in the Rite of Marriage is the consent of the couple in the presence of the Church's minister, two witnesses, and the congregation.

A husband and wife were at a party chatting with some friends when the object of marriage counseling came up. "Oh, we'll never need that. My husband and I have a great relationship," the wife explained. "He was a communications major in college and I majored in theater arts. He communicates real well and I just act like I'm listening."

- **The minister invites the couple to offer their consent, saying, "Since it is your intention to enter into marriage, join your right hands and declare your consent before God and his Church."**
- **The couple then publicly profess their consent, which is further symbolized by the blessing and exchange of rings.**
- **Although not required to do so, Catholics are encouraged to celebrate their marriage within the Eucharistic liturgy.**

So What?

So what difference does it make that Catholics celebrate the sacraments of holy orders and matrimony? It means that we recognize that "it's not about me!" These two sacraments are called the sacraments at the service of communion, and they remind us that we are all called to put aside our own needs to serve the needs of the community. In a society and culture that promotes the importance of the individual, the sacraments of holy orders and matrimony promote the importance of the community.

Scripture

But Jesus summoned them and said, "You know that the rulers of the Gentiles lord it over them, and the great ones make their authority over them felt. But it shall not be so among you. Rather, whoever wishes to be great among you shall be your servant; whoever wishes to be first among you shall be your slave. Just so, the Son of Man did not come to be served but to serve and to give his life as a ransom for many." (Matthew 20:25–28)

Prayer

Lord, Jesus, you taught us not to serve ourselves, but to serve God and others. Grant me the grace I need to be of service to others. Help me to put my own needs aside and to focus on the needs of others. Bless our Church, Lord, with good priests and healthy marriages, so that together, we may build up the community of faith and bring praise to your name. Amen.

PART THREE

The Moral Life:
Living Faith

Chapter Twelve

Handle with Care: Human Dignity, Sin, and Mercy

We tend to think of construction sites as places where the only skill needed is brute strength. By the same token, the stereotype of a construction worker is that of a gruff, grizzly, "bull-in-a-china shop" sort of guy. The truth is, many aspects of construction require precision, craftsmanship, and, dare I say it, a delicate touch. Various aspects of construction involve the use of materials that are easily damaged, if not downright fragile. The bottom line: handle with care. Human beings, though very durable, are inherently fragile, and need to be handled with care. Catholic morality guides us to show this care in all of our interactions with fellow human beings.

A Little Respect

In the classic *Charlie Brown Christmas* cartoon, a character named "Pigpen" is assigned the role of innkeeper for the group's upcoming Christmas pageant. The problem is, Pigpen has a hygiene problem, depicted by a little cloud of dust that emanates from him. Frieda, the girl playing the innkeeper's wife, complains to the director, Charlie Brown, that Pigpen's dust will ruin her naturally curly hair. Charlie does his best to assuage Frieda's fears by telling her to imagine that Pigpen's dust has some inherent value: "Don't think of it as dust. Think of it as maybe the soil of some great past civilization. Maybe ancient Babylon. It staggers the imagination. He could be carrying soil that was trod upon by Solomon or even Nebuchadnezzar." Pigpen then remarks to Frieda, "Sort of makes you want to treat me with more respect, doesn't it?"

The truth is, we tend to treat people with more respect when we perceive them to be of less-than-common origins. Who of us has not had the experience of treating someone gruffly, only to have a friend or bystander point out to us that this person was a celebrity, an entertainer, an athlete, an office-holder, or even the boss's son or daughter? If only we had recognized this person's special status!

Jesus' Parable of the Last Judgment, in Matthew 25, deals with this issue. Jesus teaches us that the key to our eternal salvation is recognizing the inherent dignity of each person we encounter in this world. This parable is creatively portrayed in the musical *Godspell.* After Jesus informs the "goats" that they are condemned for not recognizing him in the hungry, thirsty, naked, imprisoned, sick, and lost, a woman portraying one of the goats coyly responds, "Big boy, if we'd a known it was you, we'd a taken you 'round the corner for a cup of coffee!"

The challenge of Christian morality is to recognize the presence of the divine and the inherent dignity of each person we meet, so that we treat each person with the respect they deserve. The Book of Genesis clearly teaches us that God created men and women in the divine image:

> God created man in his image; in the divine image he created him; male and female he created them. (Genesis 1:27)

Because human beings continued to fail at recognizing the divine in one another, God sent his only Son, Jesus, to put a human face on the divine, enabling Jesus to say "[W]hatever you did for one of these least brothers of mine, you did for me" (Matthew 25:40). Human dignity is grounded in the fact that Jesus, through his Incarnation, death, and Resurrection, is present in every human person, including those who are hungry, thirsty, a stranger, naked, sick, or imprisoned.

> **"Attitudes of prejudice and bias against any individual for any reason, as well as actions or judgments based on prejudiced or biased views, violate God's will and law."**
>
> (*USCC for Adults,* p. 326)

Sort of makes you want to treat people with a little more respect, doesn't it?

It is because of our inherent human dignity—and especially because of the Incarnation—that love of God and love of neighbor cannot be separated.

Catholic morality is about much more than keeping good order in society, avoiding evil, and doing good. It is one of the ways we worship God. In other words, we worship God—bow to God, align ourselves with God—when we live moral lives. Catholic morality is about growing closer to God and discovering the divine within ourselves and our neighbors. We strive to do good and avoid evil, not to get God's approval or to save ourselves, but because by doing so, we align ourselves with God. When we sin, we remove ourselves from God's path and pave our own way toward other destinations that ultimately are dead ends. We are taught in kindergarten that "God is love." This sounds so simplistic and yet it is the basis of Catholic morality. When we love—truly love, selflessly—we encounter God, who is love. So, if you're looking to "have an experience of God," you won't find him unless there are other people around for you to love.

If you're looking to "have an experience of God," you won't find him unless there are other people around for you to love.

Sin

In case you haven't noticed, talking about sin has gone out of style. Although we don't want to wallow in our sinfulness, without some understanding of sin, we have no need to be saved! What we need is a healthy understanding of sin, a healthy dose of fear, a healthy dose of guilt, and above all, a healthy understanding of grace and mercy, which trump all of the above.

So let's begin our understanding of sin by talking about *grace.* Grace is not something quantifiable. It is not something that we store up. Grace is a relationship—our relationship with God. When we are in the state of grace, we are in a healthy relationship with God, filled with God's life. For example, when we say, "Hail Mary, full of grace" we are saying that Mary is filled with God's life and that she is in a deeply intimate relationship with God.

"'Behold the fowls of the air. . . . Are ye not much better than they?' Who is ye?!!"

Grace is not something that we earn. It is a gift from God. God graces us with his presence. We can either accept that relationship or we can ignore it; or worse yet, we can reject it. In Baptism, we have been gifted with God's grace. We have been welcomed into an intimate relationship with the Divine. Any discussion of sin must begin with an understanding of grace.

Grace is a relationship—our relationship with God.

Now, with grace as our backdrop, let's talk about sin. Sin is the ignoring, injuring, or rejecting of our relationship with God. Since God has indicated clearly that loving him is inseparable from love of neighbor, we know that sin is also the ignoring, injuring, or rejecting of our relationship with others.

The Seven Deadly Sins

When I was a kid, I remember going to confession with a "laundry list" of actions I had performed: I talked back to my parents, I lied to my teacher, I fought with my brothers and sisters, etc. (I just made up all of those, of course. I was an angel.) As I've grown older, I've outgrown the notion of a laundry list of sinful actions and instead have come to focus my atten-

A catechist asked her class, "Does anyone here know what we mean by sins of omission?" A small girl replied, "Aren't those the sins we should have committed, but didn't?"

Venial and Mortal Sin

When we ignore or injure our relationship with God or others, we call these sins *venial*, which means that they are less serious, but still harmful. When we reject our relationship with God and others, we call this *mortal* sin, because it "kills" the life of grace within us. For a sin to be mortal, three conditions must apply.

- it must be a very serious offense (serious matter)
- the person must know how serious the sin is (full knowledge)
- the person must freely choose to do it anyway (full consent)

Sins of Omission

Jesus provided us with a great example of the sin of omission in the Parable of the Rich Man and Lazarus (not the Lazarus he raised from the dead) in Luke 16:19-31. The rich man in the story doesn't do anything directly to harm poor Lazarus who sits at his gate. Rather, it is the fact that the rich man ignores the plight of Lazarus that makes him guilty of sin. We pray for forgiveness from sins of commission and omission at Mass when, in the Penitential Rite, we ask forgiveness, "for what I have done and for what I have failed to do."

tion on sinful attitudes. After all, sin begins in the heart and mind—only eventually (and not in all cases) is it expressed through action.

Realizing that adults can conceptualize sin in this way, the Church provides us with a description of seven sinful attitudes, known as the Seven Deadly, or Capital, Sins. We call them "deadly" or "capital" because they dull our spiritual senses, thus destroying our spiritual health. Following are the seven deadly sins, along with the corresponding virtues (sometimes called the Contrary Virtues) that help us to overcome the sin:

- **Lust**: an inordinate craving for bodily pleasures. We combat the sin of lust with the virtue of *chastity*.
- **Greed (also known as *avarice* or *covetousness*)**: the desire for possessing what we don't have simply for the sake of having it, not because we need it. We overcome greed by practicing the virtue of *generosity*.
- **Envy**: the desire for what others have simply because they have it and we don't. We defeat the sin of envy by practicing the virtue of *kindness*.
- **Gluttony**: an inordinate intake of food and drink. We combat the sin of gluttony by practicing the virtue of *temperance*.

> **"Take God for your spouse and friend and walk with Him continually, and you will not sin, will learn to love, and the things you must do will work out prosperously for you."**
>
> —St. Teresa of Ávila

- **Sloth**: a lack of effort in working at our relationship with God and others. We can counter the effects of sloth by practicing the virtue of *zeal.*
- **Anger**: a desire for vengeance that leads us to want to harm another person. We overcome anger by practicing the virtue of *gentleness.*
- **Pride**: excessive self-esteem and a desire to be noticed by others. Pride is overcome through the practice of the virtue of *humility.*

Mercy

Our discussion of sin does not end here. The first word of our discussion about sin was *grace* and the last word of this discussion is *mercy.* We begin and end with God. Sin is what gets in between grace and mercy. Unfortunately, when we think of the word *mercy,* we often think of someone groveling before an evil villain, crying out for his or her life to be spared. God's mercy does not have to be begged for. It is offered to us as a gift. *Mercy* is another word for compassion or kindness that is directed toward an offender. Mercy is what God always offers to us, despite our offenses. Sin is not the end of the story. Mercy is what awaits us. God's merciful love calls us out of sin and redeems us—saves us, delivers us—from every evil and restores us to grace. When we respond to God's mercy with repentance and contrition, we are restored to grace; our relationship with God is deepened. When we pray for God's mercy, we are praying for the grace we need to accept that which God is always offering.

Sin is what gets in between grace and mercy.

So What?

So what difference does it make that Catholics believe in human dignity, grace, sin, and mercy? It means that we see living a moral life as an act of worship. It is a way of aligning ourselves with God, who is love. It means that we cannot separate love of God and love of neighbor. Loving our neighbors is how we encounter God, in whose image we are all made. It means that we strive to treat people with respect and "handle" them with care.

Scripture

"But what comes out of a person, that is what defiles. From within people, from their hearts, come evil thoughts, unchastity, theft, murder, adultery, greed, malice, deceit, licentiousness, envy, blasphemy, arrogance, folly. All these evils come from within and they defile." (Mark 7:20–23)

Prayer

I confess to almighty God,
and to you, my brothers and sisters,
that I have sinned through my own fault
in my thoughts and in my words,
in what I have done,
and in what I have failed to do;
and I ask blessed Mary, ever virgin,
all the angels and saints,
and you, my brothers and sisters,
to pray for me to the Lord our God.

May almighty God have mercy on us,
forgive us our sins,
and bring us to everlasting life.
Amen.

Chapter Thirteen
Building according to Code: The Commandments, Beatitudes, and Virtues

One day, years ago, the apartment building my family and I grew up in literally began to fall apart, as huge bricks on the upper floors came crashing down to the ground. Over the ensuing weeks and months, building inspectors came out repeatedly to tell my parents what they needed to do to bring the building up to code. The problem was, the building was so old that it had been built before any of the codes were in effect. Bringing it up to code would be cost-prohibitive. Eventually the building had to be demolished—a good example of why codes are important to follow from the get-go. In order to align ourselves with God, we need to follow a code that God himself provides: the Ten Commandments.

The Law of Love is No Secret Code

Recently, there have been a flurry of books, such as *The Da Vinci Code* and *The Secret,* that purport to reveal life's best-kept secrets. In particular, *The Secret* suggests that the law of attraction is the key to getting everything you've ever wanted. You just need to know "the secret." Many of these books suggest that the Church is keeping secrets.

The interesting thing is the Church, and for that matter, Judaism, has been telling us for thousands of years that there is no secret to finding prosperity—and not just material prosperity—in life: the key is God's Law of Love, known to Jews and Christians alike as the Ten Commandments or the Decalogue. In the Judeo-Christian

God does not keep secrets.

tradition, there are no secrets because God does not keep secrets. In fact, there is quite the opposite: *revelation.* Life is a mystery and God is a mystery, but God reveals himself to us and reveals his Law of Love, which enables us to navigate through life. The Decalogue is our building code.

God revealed this code to Moses on the top of Mount Sinai in the midst of thunder and lightning—a *theophany* (Exodus 19). No secret there. By its very definition, a theophany is not a secret, but a revelation.

God inscribed this code—his Law of Love—on stone tablets and commanded that these be carried in the Ark of the Covenant wherever the people went. No secret there either.

In the book of Deuteronomy, God talks about his Law of Love and its conspicuousness:

> "For this command which I enjoin on you today is not too mysterious and remote for you. It is not up in the sky, that you should say, 'Who will go up in the sky to get it for us and tell us of it, that we may carry it out?' Nor is it across the sea, that you should say, 'Who will cross the sea to get it for us and tell us of it, that we may carry it out?' No, it is something very near to you, already in your mouths and in your hearts; you have only to carry it out." (Deuteronomy 30:11–14)

Once again, no secret.

Jesus continues this revelation, speaking about the "kingdom of God" (the state of life in which the Law of Love reigns over all) in the following way:

> Asked by the Pharisees when the kingdom of God would come, he said in reply, "The coming of the kingdom of God cannot be observed, and no one will announce, 'Look, here it is,' or, 'There it is.' For behold, the kingdom of God is among you." (Luke 17:20–21)

Bottom line? No secrets. Quite the contrary. The "code" we are to live by is very much an "in-your-face" reality.

God's Law of Love—The Ten Commandments

In the Gospels, we learn of a rich young man who approached Jesus and asked, "Good Teacher, what must I do to inherit eternal life?" (Mark 10:17). Like many people, this young man was searching for more. He had much but he still sought the true meaning of life that he was not finding in his possessions and status. How did Jesus respond? By telling him to *Live the commandments!*

Jesus went on to explain that to truly live the commandments means to live in an intimate relationship with the Lord—a relationship that makes all else secondary. Jesus is telling us that the commandments are not simply a list of rules to follow. They are the principles that articulate how we live in relationship with God, who alone has eternal life. In essence, the commandments are a gift.

To truly live the commandments means to live in an intimate relationship with the Lord—a relationship that makes all else secondary.

We don't normally think of rules as a gift. However, the Book of Exodus tells us that the Jewish people readily embraced the gift of the Ten Commandments.

> So Moses went and summoned the elders of the people. When he set before them all that the LORD had ordered him to tell them, the people all answered together, "Everything the LORD has said, we will do." Then Moses brought back to the LORD the response of the people. (Exodus 19:7–8)

This code revealed how they could maintain an intimate relationship with the God who liberated them from slavery. For the Jewish people—and for us Christians—the Commandments are a gift: the key to aligning ourselves with God who, despite our sinfulness, liberates us from the tyranny of sin. In response, we

"I don't remember all ten commandments, but I know I'm not supposed to take off my shoes during the service unless I just changed my socks."

Laws Set Us Free—Huh?

We tend to think of laws as restricting. To the Jewish people, however, the Decalogue was the key to maintaining their freedom. So how do laws set us free? Think of it this way: Let's say I want to be free to enjoy a good game of tennis. However, I am trapped (enslaved) by my inability to swing the racket properly. If I get coaching from a tennis pro, he or she will teach me the rules of a good tennis swing. If I follow these rules, I will be free to truly enjoy the game of tennis. In the same way, the Ten Commandments free us from enslavement to that which separates us from truly loving God and others.

follow his code so that we can continue to enjoy the grace of this saving relationship.

There's a big difference between "not breaking the commandments" and living the commandments. The Ten Commandments are truly a path for life. It is no coincidence, then, that since the earliest days of the Church, Christians taught the Ten Commandments to those who were preparing to embark upon this new "Way"—this new path of life. Since the time of St. Augustine, the Church has required those preparing for baptism to know the Ten Commandments.

There's a big difference between "not breaking the commandments" and living the commandments.

But Didn't Jesus "Change" All This?

When someone asked Jesus what the greatest commandment was, he answered that it is to love the Lord your God with all your heart, soul, mind and strength, and to love your neighbor as yourself (Mark 12:29–31). Doesn't this mean that Jesus changed everything when it comes to the Ten Commandments? On the contrary, Jesus was summing up the Ten Commandments in a nutshell: the first three commandments teach us about love of God and the next seven commandments teach us about love of neighbor. Jesus' summary of the commandments reinforces the crucial notion that love of God and love of neighbor cannot be separated. This was the message of Pope Benedict XVI's first encyclical *Deus Est Caritas*—God is love. To love God, we must love our neighbor. To love God, we must live the commandments.

But is it truly possible, in this day and age, to love God above all else and to love our neighbors as ourselves? If we know that the Ten Commandments are a gift, then we know that the answer is yes. God did not give us a gift that we could not "use." God makes it possible, through his grace and through his Son, Jesus, for us to follow his Law of Love. Drawing upon God's grace—his life within us—we can live the Law of Love each and every day. And in doing so, we can find prosperity and fulfillment.

The First Commandment ***I am the Lord your God. You shall have no other gods before me.***

St. Augustine wrote, "Our hearts are restless, Lord, until they find rest in you." The First Commandment is the key to filling the empty, restless space that we all have within ourselves. Many things hold the promise of filling that space: money, possessions, status, power, sex, drugs, alcohol, popularity, accomplishments. To have no other gods beside the one true God is to have the empty space within ourselves filled. Another way to think of it is to realize that the empty space within is not empty at all, but is the subtle indwelling of God that we all too often strive to displace with something that we think will feel better.

The Second Commandment ***You shall not take the name of the Lord your God in vain.***

The sitcom *Seinfeld* once showed Jerry trying to carry on a relationship with a woman whose name he could not remember. Needless to say, the results were comically disastrous. Revealing one's name is a crucial step in forming and deepening a relationship. The Second Commandment reminds us that God has given us his name so that we can enter into relationship with him. The Second Commandment is not limited to avoiding swearing, cursing, or using bad language. It's about living in relationship with a God who thinks enough of us to reveal his name in hopes that we might come to know him better.

The Third Commandment ***Keep holy the Sabbath day.***

Muscles actually grow not during exercise, but when the body is at rest *after* exercise, when muscle fibers that were split during exercise are restored and strengthened. Without rest, muscles will not grow. In a similar way, without rest, our spiritual muscles will not grow. Resting on the Sabbath

Two Versions of the Commandments?

You may notice that the commandments are sometimes divided and numbered differently depending on tradition—Jewish, Catholic, Orthodox, Protestant.

- The Protestant list typically divides what Catholics consider the First Commandment into two Commandments: *You shall have no other gods but me* (Protestant First Commandment) and *You shall not make unto you any graven images* (Protestant Second Commandment).
- The Protestant list then combines into the Tenth Commandment (*You shall not covet anything that belongs to your neighbor*), what Catholics consider the Ninth and Tenth Commandments.
- The Catholic Church traditionally follows the division and numbering established by St. Augustine in the fourth century.

day is all about caring for the gift of our lives. We do so by refraining from our usual productivity in order that we might recognize and appreciate the source of our productivity—God—and in doing so, be renewed.

The Fourth Commandment ***Honor your father and your mother.***

In general, people just don't like being told what to do. We all want to be independent. Unfortunately, total independence is a mirage. The essence of the spiritual life is the admission, not of independence, but of *dependence.* The Fourth Commandment is the recognition that we are not lone rangers. We are accountable to others. This accountability begins at home. The Fourth Commandment is the acknowledgment of accountability to a higher authority and the embracing of humility—the realization that we are not the final word on anything.

The Fifth Commandment ***You shall not kill.***

The Fifth Commandment is not simply about avoiding homicidal actions. It is about appreciating the very gift of life. When something is of great value we treasure it, protect it, and defend it. Human life is not ours. It is a gift from God. The Fifth Commandment is about recognizing that all human life is a gift from God, from the moment of conception to the moment of death. Yes, the Fifth Commandment is about abortion, euthanasia, and

~~nuclear war~~. But it is also about the extent to which we recognize the dignity of human life and the image of God in the person who cuts us off on the expressway, disagrees with our political stance, or has the gall to be of a different ethnic background.

The Sixth Commandment ***You shall not commit adultery.***

God invented sex. In fact, God has such high esteem for the act of sex that he gave it to the Church to be protected within the sacrament of matrimony. The Sixth Commandment is not about avoiding something bad. It is about protecting something very good and very precious. Sex between a husband and wife is the ultimate act of self-revelation. It is the ultimate expression of intimacy. In this way, it mirrors God's own self-revelation to us and God's desire to know us intimately. As sexual beings, every relationship we enter into is in some way sexual. This means that the Sixth Commandment is not just about married people having extramarital sex. It is about all of us, our relationships, and how we are to share ourselves appropriately with others.

The Seventh Commandment ***You shall not steal.***

"You can't take it with you." We use this phrase to remind ourselves that, in essence, we own nothing, but are only stewards of God's creation during our time on earth. Unfortunately, we sometimes forget this and seek to possess that which does not belong to us. The Seventh Commandment is certainly about shoplifting, embezzling, and thievery. But it is also about the sharing the goods of the earth that have been given to all but are often seen as "mine."

The Eighth Commandment ***You shall not bear false witness against your neighbor.***

Trusting others can be a challenge, especially if our trust has been shattered or shaken. In the Bible, God reveals himself as the One who can be trusted. We are accustomed to saying that "God is love" but the Bible also

A catechist was discussing the Ten Commandments with her class. After explaining the commandment to "honor thy father and thy mother," she asked "Is there a commandment that teaches us how to treat our brothers and sisters?" Without missing a beat one young boy answered, "Thou shall not kill."

teaches us "God is truth" (John 14:6). When we live in truth, we live in God. The Eighth Commandment is about more than not telling lies. It is about living in such a way that others know we can be trusted and counted on. It is not just about avoiding falsehood, but also about giving witness to and living in the Truth.

The Ninth Commandment *You shall not covet your neighbor's wife.*
We all have desires. Unfortunately, many of us have the notion that, in order to be good Catholics, we must squelch all desires. This is where so many of us walk away sad, because we continue to have desires. The truth is, Christianity is not about eliminating desires. It is about directing and mastering our desires, lest they master us. The Ninth Commandment directs us to be sure that our desires are directed toward that which the First Commandment indicated will alone satisfy us: God.

The Tenth Commandment *You shall not covet your neighbor's goods.*
When children break open a piñata, they scurry quickly to grab a big share of the candy, in doing so often playfully trampling each other. Unfortunately, as members of the human family, we often scurry to grab "our share" of the world's resources, sometimes in doing so trampling our neighbors. The Tenth Commandment calls us to an awareness of greed and envy and their deadly effects, not only on personal relationships, but on global relationships. It reminds us that we are brothers and sisters, not competitors.

The Beatitudes—The Counterintuitive Commandments

Remember our discussion of Copernicus in chapter 2? He was the sixteenth-century Polish astronomer and mathematician who proposed that the earth revolved around the sun and not the other way around. To many people of his time, his proposal was *counterintuitive*, meaning that it was contrary to what common sense suggested. According to the human eye, the sun, the moon, and the stars seemed to revolve around the earth. When Jesus taught us how to live God's Law of Love, he offered us the Beatitudes, which we can think of as the "counterintuitive commandments"—they go against common sense. This should not come as a surprise, however, since the gospel itself is counterintuitive. Does common sense teach us to love our neighbors, to pray for our persecutors, to turn the other cheek, or to find life through death? No. That's why following God's Law of Love, as taught by Jesus, calls us to conversion. We need to change the way we think. Jesus gives us the Beatitudes, a counterintuitive recipe for happiness, to help us live according to the Law of Love. While the Gospels give us two versions of the Beatitudes, Matthew 5:3–12 and Luke 6:20–26, we will use Matthew's version.

> **The word *Beatitude* refers to a state of deep happiness or joy. These Beatitudes are taught by Jesus as the foundations for a life of authentic Christian discipleship and the attainment of ultimate happiness. They give spirit to the Law of the Ten Commandments and bring perfection to moral life.**
>
> (*USCC for Adults*, pp. 308–09)

- **Blessed are the poor in spirit, for theirs is the kingdom of heaven.** Human intuition tells us that being rich is the key to happiness. Jesus reveals that those who are poor recognize their dependence on others and on God, something that wealth can prevent us from seeing.
- **Blessed are they who mourn, for they will be comforted**. Common sense tells us that experiencing sadness is bad. Jesus reveals that mourning is part of the human condition and sensitizes us to the fact that we are a people in need of God's healing.
- **Blessed are the meek, for they will inherit the land.** Human intuition tells us that the strong and the proud will prevail. Jesus reveals that the strong and the proud deceive themselves into thinking they are self-sufficient, but that the meek and humble truly recognize that God alone sustains.
- **Blessed are they who hunger and thirst for righteousness, for they will be satisfied**. Common sense dictates that I should look out for my own needs. Jesus reveals that God's will is for all people to experience justice and that when we hunger for righteousness, we align ourselves with God.
- **Blessed are the merciful, for they will be shown mercy**. Human intuition tells us that the winners in life are those who show no mercy to others on their way to the top. Jesus reveals that the heart of God is mercy and that we cannot hope to receive mercy if we do not show mercy to others.

- **Blessed are the clean of heart, for they will see God.** Common sense tells us that we should do whatever it takes to achieve our goals: the ends justify the means. Jesus reveals that our hearts—our intentions—must be transparent and pure, motivated by love.
- **Blessed are the peacemakers, for they will be called children of God.** Human intuition tells us to build walls to separate us and protect us from others. Jesus reveals that only those who build peace—who remove barriers—are truly reflecting God's image.
- **Blessed are they who are persecuted for the sake of righteousness, for theirs is the kingdom of heaven.** Common sense tells us to avoid conflict at all costs and to fly under the radar. Jesus reveals that we will be persecuted for living God's Law of Love, but that it is through this very persecution that God's greatness is made known to others.
- **Blessed are you when they insult you and persecute you and utter every kind of evil against you (falsely) because of me.** Rejoice and be glad, for your reward will be great in heaven. Human intuition demands immediate gratification. Jesus reveals that the "rewards" for following the Law of Love are much deeper than an immediate good feeling.

The Virtues

Certain behaviors, often bad ones, are habit forming. When it comes to good habits, we need to work at forming them. For centuries, the Church has taught seven habits, or principles, that are key to living as disciples of Jesus. These habits are called *virtues.* They can be referred to as habits because they need to be used; they can be lost if they are neglected.

- **Faith** is the ability to believe in God and give our lives to him. It makes us able to trust God completely and to accept all that God has revealed and taught us.
- **Hope** is the desire for all of the good things God has planned for us. Hope gives us confidence that God will always be with us and that we will live with God forever in heaven.

"What's this I hear about you practicing Christianity on company time?"

Cardinal and Theological Virtues

The first three virtues are called *theological* virtues because they come from God and lead to God. The remaining four—the *cardinal* virtues—are human virtues, acquired by education and good actions. They are named for the Latin word for "hinge" (*cardo*), meaning "that on which other things depend."

- **Charity,** also known as *love,* involves more than just feelings; it is the way we think about God and act toward him and others. Charity brings all the virtues together in perfect harmony. "So faith, hope, love remain," St. Paul writes in 1 Corinthians 13:13, "but the greatest of these is love."

> **"Sell not virtue to purchase wealth, nor liberty to purchase power."**
> —Benjamin Franklin

- **Prudence** is the ability to decide what is good and then choose to do it. It leads us to stop and think before we act.
- **Justice** is the respect we show for the rights of others, striving to give them what is rightfully theirs. The just person considers the needs of others and always tries to be fair.
- **Fortitude** is the courage to do what is right, even when it is very difficult. It provides us the strength to resist the temptations we face.
- **Temperance** is the ability to balance what we want with what we need. It helps us moderate our desires for enjoyment and builds self-control.

So What?

So what difference does it make that Catholics believe in the Ten Commandments, the Beatitudes, and the virtues? It means that we don't have to go searching for some great secret to a deeper relationship with God. God has revealed to us, through the Ten Commandments and through Jesus Christ, who is the incarnation of the Law of Love, how we are to live in order to remain in grace, in relationship with him. God's Law of Love is a gift that enables us to live a life that is blessed with God's presence.

Scripture

Asked by the Pharisees when the kingdom of God would come, he said in reply, "The coming of the kingdom of God cannot be observed, and no one will announce, 'Look, here it is,' or, 'There it is.' For behold, the kingdom of God is among you." (LUKE 17:20-21)

Prayer

Thank you, good and gracious God, for the gift of your Law of Love and for revealing the kingdom in our midst. Thank you for not keeping secrets, and for showing us how we are to live in order for us to remain in close relationship with you. Help me to love you above all else, and to love my neighbors, especially when that gets challenging. Likewise, help me to be a loveable neighbor so that others may not find in me an obstacle to a deeper relationship with you. Amen.

Chapter Fourteen
Tuck-Pointing, Painting, and Siding: Works of Mercy and Social Justice

My wife and I have owned two homes, the first of which needed painting and tuck-pointing, the second of which needed new siding. Over time, homes take a beating from the elements, and need a facelift of sorts. It's amazing what a little tuck-pointing, painting, or siding can do to improve the life and look of a home. Life has a way of taking its toll on people at times. When folks find themselves "beaten down" by life, they are in need of some tender loving care. For Catholics, the Works of Mercy and our commitment to Social Justice are ways in which we show this loving care to those who need it most.

Minding Your Own (and Others') Business

In Charles Dickens' *A Christmas Carol* (Prestwick House Inc., 2005), Ebenezer Scrooge is visited by the ghost of his former business partner, Jacob Marley, who is lamenting the fate of one who neglected the needs of his fellow human beings in life. Scrooge tries to assuage Marley by reminding him that he was always a good man of business. Marley cries out in anguish, "Business! Mankind was my business! The common welfare was my business; charity, mercy, forbearance, and benevolence were all my business."

"Business! Mankind was my business!"

Apparently, minding other people's business is our business.

Catholics have a long history of minding other people's business when that business involves showing mercy. The apostle James made it very clear that faith in Jesus must translate into good works:

> What good is it, my brothers, if someone says he has faith but does not have works? Can that faith save him? If a brother or sister has nothing to wear and has no food for the day, and one of you says to them, "Go in peace, keep warm, and eat well," but you do not give them the necessities of the body, what good is it? So also faith of itself, if it does not have works, is dead. Indeed someone might say, "You have faith and I have works." Demonstrate your faith to me without works, and I will demonstrate my faith to you from my works. (James 2:14–18)

We do not perform good works in order to please or assuage God. We do not do good works in order to earn grace or salvation. We do good works because God is love and we yearn to live in God. By sharing love with others, we encounter the living God. The Catholic Church identifies for us various works of mercy—the Corporal Works of Mercy and the Spiritual Works of Mercy—to guide and inspire us to live for others.

The Catholic Church identifies for us, various works of mercy—the Corporal Works of Mercy and the Spiritual Works of Mercy—to guide and inspire us to live for others.

The *Corporal Works of Mercy* can be traced to the Parable of the Last Judgment in Matthew 25, which we discussed in chapter 11. These works are kind acts by which we help our neighbors with their everyday material and physical needs. Here are some suggestions for how we can practice these in our everyday lives.

- **Feeding the Hungry**—Support and volunteer for food pantries, soup kitchens, and agencies that feed the hungry; make a few sandwiches to hand out as you walk through areas of your city or town where you may encounter people who are in need of food.
- **Sheltering the Homeless**—Help neighbors to care for their homes and do repairs; support and/or volunteer at a homeless shelter; support and/or volunteer for Catholic Charities initiatives, the Catholic Campaign for Human Development, and Habitat for Humanity.

- **Clothing the Naked**—Go through your drawers and closets and find good-condition clothes to donate to St. Vincent DePaul or other agencies that accept clothing; donate maternity clothes and baby clothes for low-income mothers and their babies; participate in clothing drives in your community and/or at work.
- **Visiting the Sick**—Spend quality time with those who are sick or homebound; take the time to call, send a card, or an e-mail to someone who is sick.
- **Visiting the Imprisoned**—Support and/or participate in ministries to those who are incarcerated; support programs sponsored by agencies that advocate on behalf of those who are unjustly imprisoned. Visit people "imprisoned" by loneliness, sickness, or old age.
- **Giving Alms to the Poor**—Take some small bills or loose change with you to hand out to those in need whom you might encounter on your way to work; throw your coin change into a jar and periodically donate it to a charity; if possible, make a regular monetary donation to a charity that tends to the needs of the poor.
- **Burying the Dead**—Be faithful about attending wakes/visitation; support or volunteer at a hospice; participate in a bereavement ministry; spend time with widows and widowers; take friends and relatives to visit the cemetery; support ministries that offer free Christian burials to people unable to afford them.

Faith and Works

For centuries, Catholics and Protestants differed on the role that performing good works plays in our salvation (justification). Protestants insisted that we are saved (justified) by faith alone. Catholics have always insisted that we are saved by faith, but that faith must be accompanied by good works. Differences such as these led Catholics and Protestants to condemn one another's teachings in the sixteenth century. In 1999, the Catholic Church and the Lutheran World Federation reached agreement on a *Joint Declaration on the Doctrine of Justification*, which revokes these condemnations while admitting that some differences about our understandings of justification remain.

A catechist taught his third-grade class about the Corporal Works of Mercy. One boy decided that he would look for the first opportunity to help the poor. That Sunday, as they were leaving church after Mass, the boy overheard his parents talking. He quickly reached into his pocket and pulled out a dollar bill. As they approached the pastor at the door, the boy offered him the dollar. The puzzled priest asked the boy what the dollar was for. The boy responded, "I'm practicing a Corporal Work of Mercy, Father. I heard my Dad say that you're the poorest preacher he's ever known, so I thought I would offer my help."

The Church also identifies works of mercy that tend to the emotional and spiritual needs of people. These are called the *Spiritual Works of Mercy.* These works are listed here along with suggestions for practicing them in everyday life.

- **Instructing**—Commit yourself to learning about the Catholic faith and share your understanding of the faith with your children and with those who welcome it; share your insights, knowledge, and skills with others, especially coworkers; take time to "tutor" those who are just beginning tasks such as a new job or parenting; read good literature and encourage others to do so.
- **Advising**—Be courageous, yet compassionate, in calling people and institutions to be faithful to Gospel values; intervene in situations in which people are clearly doing harm to themselves or others; respond to negative and prejudicial comments with positive statements; put an end to gossip by walking away; set a good example for others.
- **Consoling**—Strive to be optimistic and to avoid cynicism; respond to cynicism, skepticism, and doubt with hope; be articulate about your own hopes; ask people about their hopes and support them in striving to attain them.
- **Comforting**—Walk with others through their pain; offer words of encouragement to those who seem discouraged; offer positive words to coworkers who are having a difficult time with their tasks; be present to those who are struggling or in emotional pain or despair; offer sympathy to those who are grieving.

- **Forgiving**—Pray for those who have wronged you and pray for the courage to forgive; ask forgiveness from others; let go of grudges; go out of your way to be positive with someone you are having a difficult time with.
- **Bearing Wrongs Patiently**—Strive to be less critical of others; overlook minor flaws and mistakes; give people the benefit of the doubt; assume that people who may have hurt you did so because they are enduring pain of their own; pray for those who have wronged you.

The key to all of the works of mercy is that these are not the sorts of actions that happen by accident. In order for them to happen, we need to be proactive. The goal of all of the Works of Mercy is to bring about a transformation in society—a transformation that reflects how God intends for us to live with one another. God's merciful love is transforming. When we share that merciful love with others, we share in God's work of transforming the world.

The goal of all of the works of mercy is to bring about a transformation in society—a transformation that reflects how God intends for us to live with one another.

Social Justice—Isn't That for Activists?

When we speak of transforming the world through our actions, we inevitably move toward the concept of *social justice.* Social justice is about people living in right relationship with God and with one another. One look at our world reveals that our relationships are not in order. So what is an individual to do about this? We are called to be aware of how our actions affect our neighbors and to respond with compassion and generosity to meet the needs of others. Social justice is the gospel in action. By virtue of our baptism, we are all called to activism—an activism that is motivated

"An awareness of the social dimension of human life is an important principle in understanding Christian morality, especially in light of the great emphasis on individualism in our society."
(*USCC for Adults*, p. 325)

Distribution of Wealth

Consider the following illustration. If you had 100 pennies to represent all of the world's wealth and 100 people to represent the population of the world, 25 people, representing all of the developed countries of the world, would share 81 pennies while 75 people, representing the rest of the world's population, would share 19 pennies, or just over two-tenths of a penny each.

not by anger or vengeance, but by love. Social justice begins with a spiritual conversion. Before we seek to change civil laws, we must first ourselves be conformed to God's Law of Love. The key to social justice is to keep in mind the common good. We are baptized into a community, the Church, which is a sign to the world of the community that all humans are called to live in. In all of our actions and relationships, we are to ask ourselves if we are acting for the common good and respecting the human dignity of others.

Catholic Social Teaching

The Catholic Church has a long tradition of applying the gospel to various situations in society, in order that society may be transformed. We call this tradition Catholic Social Teaching. Here is an overview of the principles of Catholic Social Teaching, as outlined by the United States Conference of Catholic Bishops.

"Justice and power must be brought together, so that whatever is just may be powerful, and whatever is powerful may be just."
BLAISE PASCAL

- **Life and Dignity of the Human Person**—Because all human life is sacred, we are called to respect and value people over material goods and to ask whether our actions respect or threaten the life and dignity of the human person.
- **Call to Family, Community, and Participation**—Our faith and our society rely upon healthy families and healthy communities. Because the family is the central social institution of our society, it must be supported and strengthened.

- **Rights and Responsibilities**—Not only does every person have a right to life, but also a right to those things needed for human decency. We are called to protect these basic human rights in order to build a healthy society.

- **Option for the Poor and Vulnerable**—It is a simple fact that in our world, many people are very rich while at the same time others are extremely poor. We are called to make a specific effort to ensure that those who are poor and vulnerable are able to meet their immediate material needs.

> **The Catholic Church has a long tradition of applying the gospel to various situations in society in order that society may be transformed.**

- **The Dignity of Work and the Rights of Workers**—Workers have basic rights that must be respected. These include: the right to productive work, to fair wages, to private property, to organize and join unions, and to pursue economic opportunity. Our Catholic faith teaches us that people do not serve the economy, but rather, the economy is meant to serve people.

- **Solidarity**—Because God is our Father, we are all brothers and sisters, with the responsibility to care for one another. Solidarity is the attitude that leads Christians to share spiritual and material goods and to recognize our interdependence.

- **Care for God's Creation**—God is the creator of all people and all things, and he wants us to enjoy his creation. We are called to make good choices—moral and ethical—that protect the ecological balance of all of God's creation.

So What?

So what difference does it make that Catholics believe in works of mercy and social justice? It means that we do not see salvation as a "God and me" reality. We recognize that God's covenant is with a people—not with individuals. It means that we see

"There! That takes care of social concerns for this year."

both sin and salvation as social realities. It means that we are to recognize our solidarity with all people, and that by engaging others with mercy, we share in God's work of transforming the world.

Scripture

"But a Samaritan traveler who came upon him was moved with compassion at the sight. He approached the victim, poured oil and wine over his wounds and bandaged them. Then he lifted him up on his own animal, took him to an inn and cared for him. The next day he took out two silver coins and gave them to the innkeeper with the instruction, 'Take care of him. If you spend more than what I have given you, I shall repay you on my way back.' Which of these three, in your opinion, was neighbor to the robbers' victim?" He answered, "The one who treated him with mercy." Jesus said to him, "Go and do likewise." (LUKE 10:33–37)

Prayer

Father, Son, and Holy Spirit, you live in loving relationship with one another. Holy Trinity, help me to live in loving relationship with others, sharing your merciful love with those who are most in need of it. Help me to hear the cries of those who are deprived of what they need to reach their fulfillment. Grant that I may unselfishly share with others, tending to their physical and spiritual needs and cooperating with you in transforming the world through your merciful love. Amen.

Chapter Fifteen
Measure Twice, Cut Once: Conscience and Moral Decision Making

One of the most well-known phrases in the construction world is "measure twice, cut once." The wisdom of this saying is grounded in common sense: poor measurements will lead to wasted materials. The message is clear: think before you act. As followers of Jesus, we are called to act in certain ways. Catholic Tradition teaches us how to think before we act.

Where Have You Gone, Jiminy Cricket?

We seem to admire people who, looking back on their lives, say, "I have no regrets." Their attitude shows that they have not, and will not, allow themselves to be handicapped by guilt and remorse. At the same time, when judges are handing down sentences to convicted criminals, they usually take into consideration whether or not the criminal shows any signs of remorse. Seeing no signs of remorse, the judge is more than likely to hand down a harsher sentence. So are guilt, remorse, and regret unhealthy states of mind that paralyze us and keep us from growing, or are they healthy attitudes that put us more deeply in touch with our human frailties?

"Aren't you supposed to take the beam out of your own eye first?"

The answer, of course, is *both.* Guilt, remorse, and regret are all functions of the human conscience. In the right measure, they can be healthy responses to our faults and limitations, and they guide our future actions. In the extreme, they can be crippling attitudes that prevent us from enjoying fullness of life. *Conscience* is a gift that can guide us through life. Properly formed, a conscience can help us choose before we act and can help us evaluate after we have acted.

Properly formed, a conscience can help us choose before we act and can help us evaluate after we have acted.

In the Disney story of *Pinocchio,* Jiminy Cricket represents Pinocchio's conscience. Balanced atop Pinocchio's shoulder, Jiminy Cricket offered guidance to the wooden boy who is trying to become human. This is a nice image, but in reality, the human conscience is not so much a voice as it is a set of eyeglasses. We do not necessarily hear a voice telling us what is right or what is wrong, but we become capable of seeing as God sees. For many of us, our physical eyesight is in need of correction. Eyeglasses, contacts, or laser surgery can correct our vision and help us to see as we were meant to see. In a similar way, our consciences—our inner eyes—must be corrected or formed so that they are aligned with the way God sees. Conscience formation, a process that was begun by our parents and teachers in our infancy, is our ongoing responsibility. A fully-formed conscience allows us to be a fully formed human being.

A good conscience requires lifelong formation.
(*USCC for Adults,* p. 314)

Back in chapter 4 we talked about how many of us bear a family resemblance to relatives, and how we are called to bear a "family resemblance" to God—Father, Son, and Holy Spirit—in whose image we are made. This notion of a family resemblance is the basis of living a moral life, because we are also called to recognize how *others* bear a resemblance

"He who sacrifices his conscience to ambition burns a picture to obtain the ashes."
—Chinese Proverb

to God. When we recognize that all people are made in the divine image, we are compelled to treat them with the dignity they deserve. A fully-formed conscience enables us to see as God sees, allowing us to recognize the divine presence in all people and to act accordingly.

Forming One's Conscience

The Church understands that we must always obey the certain judgment of our own consciences. So how do we form a conscience? Here are some basic ways

- learning from our mistakes and those of others
- praying for guidance
- reading and listening to Scripture
- learning about the teachings of the Church
- considering the effects of our actions on others

What Were You Thinking?

Babe Ruth, Mickey Mantle, Ernie Banks, Wilt Chamberlain, Joe Namath, Bobby Hull—some of the greatest athletes in their respective sports, who all have one thing in common: they never were asked to coach or manage a team. Why? It's because they relied on sheer physical talent to succeed in their respective sports more than they relied on thinking. Mickey Mantle himself was quoted as saying, "I could never be a manager. All I have is natural ability." Often the best coaches and managers are those former players who, in many respects, struggled to succeed because their abilities were limited. They relied on thinking, and as a result they became students of the game they once played, enabling them to later manage others.

A sportsman, who happened to be Catholic, ignored his conscience and decided to go bear-hunting on Sunday instead of going to Mass, even though he knew this was wrong. His conscience was bothering him as he entered the woods, when suddenly he heard some rustling nearby. He quickly tried to raise his rifle to shoot, but alas, the large grizzly was upon him. As the huge bear was squeezing the life out of him, the hunter prayed with his last breath, "Please, God, turn this bear into a good Catholic." Immediately, the bear released him, knelt down, made the Sign of the Cross with a large paw, and prayed, "Bless us, O Lord, and these thy gifts, which we are about to receive . . ."

Now, back to real life. Parents occasionally find themselves asking their children, "What were you thinking?" after they've discovered their children doing something foolish. The question implies, of course, that there wasn't much thinking going on at all. Unfortunately, while parents are trying to teach their kids to think, society is teaching them that, "if it feels good, do it." The problem, of course, is that life requires thinking. St. Augustine pointed this out very clearly when he wrote, "No one believes anything unless one first thought it believable. . . . Everything that is believed is believed after being preceded by thought. . . . Not everyone who thinks believes, since many think in order not to believe; but everyone who believes thinks, thinks in believing and believes in thinking" (*Predestination of the Saints* 5, PL 44:962-63).

Author Robert Louis Wilken notes that "For Christians, thinking is a part of believing" (*The Spirit of Early Christian Thought,* Yale University Press, New Haven & L London, 2003). We are called to love the Lord God with our entire heart, soul, mind, and strength. Notice that the *mind* is included. Yes, love requires thinking. This means that the choices and decisions we make in life require thinking. What kind of thinking goes into making a good moral choice? Although the choices themselves are not easy, the steps involved are. The morality of any act has three dimensions to be considered.

The morality of any act has three dimensions to be considered: the object chosen, the intention, and the circumstances

- **The object chosen** (What am I choosing to do?)—If the object is an evil action, such as killing innocent people, the act as a whole is wrong no matter how good the intention is.
- **The intention** (Why am I choosing this action?)—A good intention does not justify an evil action. The end does not justify the means. If the object is a good action, but the intention is to make someone else look bad, the act as a whole is wrong.
- **The circumstances of the action** (When, how, and where am I performing this action?)—Circumstances play a role in determining moral culpability. To betray military secrets is wrong, but if that betrayal occurs at gunpoint, the person's culpability is lessened. Under the wrong circumstances, a good object done with the right intention can

be wrong. For example, doing an archeological dig to learn more about various cultures is a good object done with the right intentions. If the dig disturbs sacred burial grounds belonging to a particular culture, however, the action becomes tainted.

Catholicism involves a great deal of thinking. Author Stephen Prothero (*Religious Literacy: What Every American Needs to Know—and Doesn't,* Harper, San Francisco, 2007) tells us that many segments of evangelical Christianity, in an attempt to forge Christian political alliances, are paying less attention to the mind—ignoring their intellectual and theological differences—and are paying more attention to the heart by emphasizing family values. As a result, many Christians love God with their hearts, but it is at the expense of their minds. Meanwhile, Catholicism reminds us that we are called to love God with our heart, soul, mind, and strength—a synthesis of reason and emotion. We are called to think before we act and, in order to think properly, we need to have a fully formed conscience. Following Jesus is indeed a choice of the heart but that choice is not made based on feelings alone. Jesus made it quite clear that following him requires thinking when he said,

Following Jesus is indeed a choice of the heart but that choice is not made based on feelings alone.

> Which of you wishing to construct a tower does not first sit down and calculate the cost to see if there is enough for its

Lifelong Learning

Because Catholics know that following Jesus requires faith and reason, we strive to continue learning about our faith throughout our entire lives. For too many of us, our confirmation in junior high or high school symbolized our "graduation" from religious education. The foundations of a sound conscience are indeed formed in the early years of our lives, however, consciences have insatiable appetites and need to be fed throughout life. The most effective way to continue nourishing our consciences is through lifelong catechesis—a commitment to learning about how God is calling us to follow Jesus in the face of today's circumstances.

completion? Otherwise, after laying the foundation and finding himself unable to finish the work the onlookers should laugh at him and say, "This one began to build but did not have the resources to finish." (Luke 14:28–30)

In other words, Jesus is telling us that we need to think.

So What?

So what difference does it make that Catholics believe in having a fully formed conscience and in making good moral decisions? It means that we are called to be thinkers. It means that we are called to lifelong catechesis. Catechesis is a huge part of being Catholic, because following Jesus is an eyes-wide-open experience. Our faith in Jesus is not blind faith. On the contrary, our faith calls us to have our eyesight corrected, so that we learn to see as God sees.

Scripture

The aim of this instruction is love from a pure heart, a good conscience, and a sincere faith. Some people have deviated from these and turned to meaningless talk, wanting to be teachers of the law, but without understanding either what they are saying or what they assert with such assurance. . . . I entrust this charge to you, Timothy, my child, in accordance with the prophetic words once spoken about you. Through them may you fight a good fight by having faith and a good conscience. Some, by rejecting conscience, have made a shipwreck of their faith. (1 TIMOTHY 1:5–7, 18–19)

Prayer

Loving God, send your Holy Spirit to ignite my heart with your love, and to open my mind so that I might follow you more closely. Help me to inform my conscience so that I can come to see myself, others, and the world as you see them. Guide me in my choices. Help me to think, so that I might act according to your will. Help me to love you with my whole heart, soul, mind, and strength. Amen.

PART FOUR

PRAYER:
PRAYING FAITH

Chapter Sixteen

Excavators and Cranes: Prayer

Building up usually is preceded by digging down. The first pieces of equipment on a construction site are usually the excavators and diggers. These tractors break up the earth and dig down, creating the space needed to lay a solid foundation, while also hauling away debris. Then, as the construction takes place, the excavators give way to cranes that are needed to reach the heights of the new construction. In our prayer lives we seek to reach new heights, but we begin by digging down. By "breaking up the ground," we are able to create the space needed for God to build us up so that we can attain heaven.

Prayer Is Not "E.T. Phone Home"

In Steven Spielberg's movie, *E.T.—The Extra-Terrestrial,* we learn about an alien creature who gets left behind on earth after his fellow explorers hurriedly blast off to return home. Although the lovable little creature is befriended by a young boy named Elliot, E.T. still wants nothing more than to return home. In order to do so, he assembles some primitive technology so that he can "phone home." In the end, he successfully contacts his home planet and a ship is sent to rescue him and take him home amidst tearful goodbyes from Elliot and his family and friends.

Nice story. Good movie. Unfortunately, the dynamic in this movie—a lost creature seeking to get the attention of those who can save him—is the same dynamic that many of us bring to the concept of prayer. We see ourselves as lost and abandoned, separated from God by our sinfulness. To bridge the gap between ourselves and God, we strive to pray, in hopes of getting God's attention so that he will draw near to us and save us. We just have to find the right way to pray and pray hard enough and our prayers will be answered, just like E.T.'s plea was answered.

Fortunately for us, prayer cannot be compared to "E.T. phone home." We have the dynamic completely backwards and upside-down. We don't need to do a thing to get God's attention. On the contrary, God is actively seeking to get our attention. As we mentioned earlier in chapter two, God takes the initiative and we are invited to respond.

All prayer, then, is a response to God.

The first time I heard this phrase, uttered by one of my professors, I objected, saying, "That can't be applied to prayer of petition. *We* initiate those prayers and we look for God to respond." My professor gave me that smile that professors use when they know they're right and you're wrong. He then went on to explain, "The only reason we are offering petitions to God in the first place is because we have seen, heard, and experienced God's saving deeds and, *in response,* we are asking for one thing more."

All prayer, then, is a response to God.

He was right and I was wrong. That explanation has made all the difference in the world to me in terms of understanding my place before God. You and I are not traveling beneath God's radar, out of his range of awareness, and in need of attracting his attention. Rather, God is actively pursuing us, inviting us to recognize his loving presence in the midst of our everyday lives. Prayer is our awareness of the divine presence in our lives. Prayer is our response to God's undying efforts to reach our hearts.

It is only with such an understanding of prayer that we can hope to achieve St. Paul's directive to "pray without ceasing" (1 Thessalonians 5:17). If prayer were simply talking to God, the only way to "pray without ceasing" would be for us to be incessantly talking to God. No relationship can survive if one person is constantly talking. Likewise, in the course of our daily lives, we simply cannot carry on an unending monologue with God. Prayer does involve talking to God, but much more than that, prayer describes all of our efforts to recognize and respond to God's presence.

Saint Ignatius of Loyola taught that with the proper mindset and awareness, we can begin to recognize God in all things, allowing all of God's creation to "speak" to us of the divine presence. Such prayer, while it may involve words, also transcends words. (More about this in the next chapter)

Basic Ways of Praying

Our communications with others take many forms. Sometimes we make small talk. Other times, we discuss business. Still other times, we share intense personal issues. Our communication with God—our prayer—also includes a variety of forms. The Church identifies the following forms of prayer:

- **Adoration**—acknowledging God's greatness
- **Petition**—asking God to address our personal needs
- **Intercession**—praying on behalf of the needs of others
- **Thanksgiving**—thanking God for all good gifts
- **Praise**—joyfully acknowledging that God is God

The *Catechism of the Catholic Church* describes prayer as "the raising of one's mind and heart to God" (2559). If these words sound familiar, perhaps you're thinking of the preface dialogue of the Mass, when the priest invites us to "Lift up your hearts" and we respond, "We lift them up to the Lord."

"The Holy Spirit taught the Church the life of prayer and led her to deeper insights into basic ways of praying: adoration, petition, intercession, thanksgiving, and praise."

(USCC for Adults, p. 467)

Just what does it mean to "lift up" our hearts? First, we need to understand that in ancient times, the heart was understood as more than a muscle pumping blood and more than a metaphor for the focal point of human emotions. To the ancient mind, the heart was the seat of all knowledge, and "to know" in biblical thinking carries the connotation of "being joined with," as a husband and wife are joined in sexual union. Second, the notion of "lifting" obviously implies that something needs to be raised or picked up from a lower level to a higher level. To lift up our hearts, then, is to *raise our knowing* from the level of self-centeredness to the level of God-centeredness. To lift up our hearts means to be joined with God—to be in communion with God.

Thus, when we speak of the "power of prayer," we are not speaking of any power that we ourselves have or even acquire as the result of praying. What we are saying is that when we join with God, we open ourselves up to the divine life within us that transforms us and empowers us to live to our full human potential. Prayer lifts us up from knowing only despair, cynicism, fear, and emptiness to knowing fullness of life, faith, hope, and love.

To pray without ceasing, then, means to live our lives in communion with God. It means to live every moment of our lives in the context of God—fully aware of God's presence in the moment. Sometimes those moments will evoke words in us. Most of the time, however, those moments are simply a silent acknowledgment of the divine presence.

To pray without ceasing, then, means to live our lives in communion with God.

Pray for Victory!

Not so long ago, during the NBA (National Basketball Association) Finals, a newspaper featured a story about a community of nuns who were praying for their local team to win the championship. Stories such as this pop up from time to time during the World Series, the Super Bowl, the Stanley Cup Playoffs, and any other major sport you can name. It makes for a cute story. Everyone wants to have God on their side. What better way then to have nuns praying for you?

Personally, I find these types of stories troublesome. The purpose of prayer is not to influence God. Prayer does not change God. Prayer changes us. No doubt, there were nuns from the opposing city praying for their local team to win the NBA Finals that same year. Do we really think that God is weighing his options, deciding which team to lead to victory based on the quality of prayers? Of course not. Now, however, the question arises: "So then, why pray at all?"

In fact, we must ask: Should we pray

- **for rain during a drought?**
- **for no rain during a parade?**
- **for teams to win a game?**
- **for the healing of a sick person?**
- **for help in passing an exam?**
- **for peace in the world?**

The answer is a resounding, "Yes, yes, YES!" However, we must know *what* we are praying for and know *why* we pray. We pray for one reason only: to align ourselves with God's will. In each of these situations, we are praying about something very important to us, seeking to align our will with God's. No matter how the situation turns out, God intervenes because God is *always* intervening. Unfortunately, however, we tend to recognize only that intervention when God's will seemingly conforms to our own and we proclaim a miracle. Miracles do indeed occur; however, Jesus himself pointed out that the greatest miracle is the transformation of a human heart. When Jesus was asked to heal a paralytic, he responded first by saying to the man, "[Y]our sins are forgiven" (Matthew 9:2). When people protested that only God can forgive sins, Jesus asked, "Which is easier, to say 'Your sins are forgiven,' or 'Rise and walk'?" (Matthew 9:5). Jesus was pointing out that the forgiveness of sin—the transformation of this man's heart—was a greater miracle than the healing of this man's paralysis. The physical healing, which was the visible miracle, is an outward sign of the greater invisible miracle—the healing of a human heart. And so, we pray

- **for rain during a drought; and if it does not rain, we continue to pray so that we can learn what God's will is for us during this challenging time.**
- **for our favorite team to win, knowing that what we are really praying for is that they will play to the best of their ability and that the outcome will be decided based on which team is better on that day (God does not decide on the outcomes of games). And if our team loses, we continue to pray to help us accept loss, to learn from it, to grow from it, and to move on with the right attitude.**

- **for a sick relative who is dying of cancer. Our deepest desire is for that person to be well. And if the person dies, we bow before the mystery of life and death and continue to pray, asking God to help us grieve, to comfort us, and to help us see that death is not the end.**
- **for help on an exam; not in place of studying, but in order to fully utilize the gift of our minds.**
- **for world peace, because we know that it is God's will and that any lack of peace is the result of human failure.**

In other words, in every situation that we pray, we are seeking to get in touch with our deepest and truest desires, to share them with God, and to align ourselves with his will, which is always for us to draw closer to him.

In every situation that we pray, we are seeking to get in touch with our deepest and truest desires, to share them with God, and to align ourselves with his will, which is always for us to draw closer to him.

So Why Does God Allow Evil to Happen?

Sometimes when bad things happen, such as the death of a loved one, others will seek to console the grieving by saying, "It's God's will." It's not much consolation to know that God is the cause of our suffering. The truth is, God does not will human suffering. Some human suffering, such as

> A Catholic pastor rallied his parishioners to pray that a tavern not be allowed to open right across the street from the church. Lo and behold, a day before the tavern was to open for business, it was struck by lightning and burned to the ground. The parishioners were satisfied with the results until the bar owner sued the parish on the grounds that the parish was ultimately responsible for the demise of his building because of their prayer campaign. In court, the parish vehemently denied all responsibility or any connection to the building's demise. The judge hearing the case commented, "I don't know how I'm going to decide this, but it appears that we have a bar owner that believes in the power of prayer, and an entire church congregation that doesn't!"

sickness and death, are part of the human condition, the result of our fall from grace, and not the punishment for any one individual's sinful life. Some suffering is brought about directly by human sinfulness, when human beings hurt other human beings. God does not will for that suffering to happen, but has given us the free will to choose between good and evil. Sometimes, when people choose evil, we are the victims. Finally, God does not will for natural disasters to hurt and kill people. Yet God's gift of creation includes the laws of physics, which do not suspend themselves when humans are caught in the path of destruction. Where is God when all this suffering is happening? He is present with us, just as he was present with his Son, Jesus, as he hung upon the cross. His presence in times of suffering enables us to see beyond the moment that we do not understand, to a moment when we will find redemption—a transformed way of seeing that brings us closer to him and thus, to our salvation. This is why Catholics prominently display crucifixes: we recognize that all suffering, like Jesus' suffering on the cross, has a redemptive aspect. In difficult times, we join our suffering with Jesus' suffering on the cross and place our faith in the promise of new life.

What about Job?

Doesn't the Book of Job answer all of our questions about prayer and suffering? Actually, no, it doesn't. The Book of Job describes the reality of suffering and illustrates various human responses. In the end, however, the book of Job tells us that suffering is part of the mystery of life and that we cannot hope to fully understand it. The Book of Job ultimately inspires us to bow our heads in the midst of suffering and to turn to God, who alone can comfort and redeem us.

"I have been driven many times to my knees by the overwhelming conviction that I had absolutely no other place to go."

–Abraham Lincoln

So What?

So what difference does it make that Catholics believe in prayer? It means that we are confident that we are not alone—God is with us. It means that we recognize that we don't have to get God's attention. Rather, we know that God is constantly seeking our attention and inviting us to respond. It means that we are in a loving relationship with the Divine, and that through this relationship we can grow in holiness. It means that God gives us the help we need to dig deep within ourselves and then lift our hearts and minds to him.

Scripture

I raise my eyes toward the mountains. From where will my help come? My help comes from the LORD, the maker of heaven and earth. God will not allow your foot to slip; your guardian does not sleep. Truly, the guardian of Israel never slumbers nor sleeps. (PSALM 121:1–4)

Prayer

Loving God, thank you for inviting me into relationship with you. Help me to recognize this invitation and to respond with humble thankfulness each and every day. Holy Spirit, teach me to pray so that I may grow closer to the Father through Jesus. Help me to not only talk to God but to listen to the ways that God is speaking to me. Amen.

Chapter Seventeen

Walkie-Talkies: Forms of Prayer

Nowadays, on construction sites, it is very common to see workers communicating with one another and with their bosses through a variety of means. Some rely on walkie-talkies. Others are on their cell phones. Still others have head sets while some have laptop computers with wireless Internet connections. Of course, some rely on the most traditional form of communication: shouting! Communication at the construction site is key to getting the job done correctly according to the architect's specs. In our prayer lives, we have many forms of communication available to us, all designed to serve one purpose: to keep us in touch with the architect of life and to align ourselves with his blueprint.

From Cell Phones to Porch Swings

Picture a very young couple, about seventeen or eighteen years old, deeply in love. They can generally be found talking to one another at great length. When they aren't with each other, they may spend hours on the phone with one another talking. When they aren't talking to each other on the phone, they're text messaging one another. Now picture an elderly couple, perhaps in their seventies, married for about fifty years. You can find them sitting on their porch swing, in perfect silence, swaying gently back and forth . . . barely a word passing between them over the course of several hours. Which couple is communicating more?

If communication is seen as strictly the passing of words between parties, then no doubt the young couple would seem to be communicating more. If, however, communication is seen as something much deeper,

"Thelma? You'll never guess who needs our prayers and why!"

something beyond words, then it's possible that the older couple is communicating more than the younger couple. The bottom line is, *both* couples are communicating, simply at different levels—ranging from the vocal level of communication to a more subtle, yet very real, form of communication that goes beyond words. Is one form of communication better than the other? No. They are just different.

This is how the Catholic Church understands the communication that takes place within prayer. Prayer can and does take many forms, ranging from vocal prayer, which is the reliance on words, to what we know as contemplative prayer—a prayer that goes beyond words. No one form of prayer is better or more effective than another. They are just different forms of communication between us and God. Much of how we pray has to do with our age and our place in life. When we are younger or just beginning to experience prayer, we tend to rely on the vocal, using words to talk to God. As we grow older, or if we have become more experienced at the practice of prayer, we may find ourselves relying less on words and yet still communicating with God. Neither form is better than the other. They are just different ways of being in communion with God who himself speaks to us in a myriad of ways.

Prayer can and does take many forms, ranging from vocal prayer, which is the reliance on words, to what we know as contemplative prayer—a prayer that goes beyond words.

Expressions of Prayer

Non-Catholics who occasionally attend Mass are often intrigued by what we Catholics "do" there. In particular, they often want to know, "what's that thing you do right before the Gospel?" when they see us quickly move our thumbs from our forehead, to our mouth, to our chest. They are fascinated to learn that we are making the Sign of the Cross over our forehead, lips, and heart, while silently praying, "May the word of God be in my mind, on my lips, and in my heart." Mind, lips, and heart—these are the three "venues," so to speak, of prayer.

Mind, lips, and heart—these are the three "venues," so to speak, of prayer.

- **vocal (lips)**
- **meditative (mind)**
- **contemplative (heart)**

Vocal Prayer

Vocal prayer, using words either spoken out loud or in the silence of our hearts, is the most natural form of prayer. For most people, it is the place where prayer begins. We can speak to God using our own words or using the words of traditional prayers.

- **Traditional Prayers**

  Traditional prayers are like family heirlooms that have been handed down to us by the Church through the centuries. Traditional prayers are helpful for the times when we cannot find words of our own to pray. They also enable groups of people to pray together in unison. Some of the best-known examples include
  - Sign of the Cross
  - Lord's Prayer (Our Father)
  - Hail Mary
  - Doxology (Glory Be to the Father)
  - Grace Before and After Meals
  - Act of Contrition
  - Peace Prayer of Saint Francis
  - Memorare
  - *Salve, Regina* (Hail, Holy Queen)
  - Prayer to the Holy Spirit

  The Liturgy of the Hours, mentioned earlier, is also a form of vocal prayer.

- **Spontaneous Prayer**

  With our rich treasury of traditional prayers, Catholics are sometimes unfamiliar with spontaneous prayer. Praying spontaneously is not as hard as it seems. The following steps are helpful:

A catechist asked her class of young children to write short prayers about anything for which they wanted to pray. As she walked around the room observing their work, she noticed one young girl writing the alphabet over and over again. The catechist asked, "Nicole, what are you doing?" Nicole responded, "I'm writing my prayer, but I couldn't think of what I wanted to say. So I'm just writing all of the letters of the alphabet, and God can put them together however he thinks best."

- Address God: God answers to many names, so any title of honor will do. For example, Dear God, Heavenly Father, Almighty God, Dear Jesus, Creator of All Things, or Loving God.
- Talk to God about the following four things. I call it the **G.I.F.T.** of prayer.

The G.I.F.T. of Prayer

> **G**ive thanks
> **I**dentify Needs
> **F**orgive and Be Forgiven
> **T**hink of Others

1. **G**ive Thanks: Being thankful reminds us that God has taken the first step and we are now responding. Offer thanks for simple things.
2. **I**dentify Your Needs: Tell God what you are worried about or concerned with, and ask for the grace you need to cope or to rise up to a challenge.
3. **F**orgive and Be Forgiven: Ask for forgiveness for any wrongs you have committed. Pray for the grace to forgive others.
4. **T**hink of Others: We never simply pray for ourselves, but we think of the needs of others.

- Conclude: Connect your prayer to Jesus by praying, "through Christ our Lord" or "in Jesus' name", "Amen."

The above formula can be used if you are asked to offer a spontaneous prayer orally on behalf of a group of people. Simply adapt *I* and *F* to be about the group, rather than about yourself.

Meditation

Meditation, or reflective prayer, is thinking about God—often with the aid of a Scripture passage, an inspirational reading, or sacred images. When we meditate, we attempt to become aware of—and "plug into"—God's power and presence in our lives.

Daily Examen

Saint Ignatius of Loyola developed a simple method of meditation by which we can review each day in order to recognize how God is active in our daily lives. Follow these steps:

- Set aside 10–15 minutes. Quiet yourself and recall God's presence, thanking God for his love and asking the Holy Spirit for guidance.
- Review your day, thanking God for the ways he blessed you this day.
- Review your day again, thinking about the opportunities you had to use the gifts God has given you, identifying the times you either did or didn't.
- Thank God for the ways you grew closer to him and ask forgiveness for the opportunities you missed or rejected.
- Resolve to cooperate with God's grace in the day(s) to come and conclude with the Lord's Prayer.

The Rosary

The Rosary combines vocal prayer with meditation that leads to contemplation. While praying the words of the Lord's Prayer, the Hail Mary, and the Glory Be to the Father, we are meditating on events in the lives of Jesus and his mother, Mary.

A Rosary consists of a string of beads and a crucifix. We begin praying the Rosary by holding the crucifix in our hands as we pray the Sign of the Cross and the Apostles' Creed.

Following the crucifix, there is

- a single bead: pray the Lord's Prayer
- a set of three beads: pray a Hail Mary at each, asking for an increase in faith, hope, and love, followed by the Glory Be to the Father
- another single bead: think about the first mystery and pray the Lord's Prayer

Next, there is a medal, followed by

- five sets of ten beads (each set is called a decade)

- a single bead between each decade, on which we think about the next mystery and pray the Lord's Prayer

We pray a Hail Mary on each bead of a decade as we reflect on a particular mystery in the lives of Jesus and Mary. Pray the Glory Be to the Father at the end of each decade.

We end by holding the crucifix as we pray the Sign of the Cross and then pray the Hail, Holy Queen.

The Church provides us with four sets of mysteries to reflect on:

- **The Joyful Mysteries** (prayed on Mondays and Saturdays)
  The Annunciation
  The Visitation
  The Nativity
  The Presentation
  The Finding of Jesus in the Temple

- **The Luminous Mysteries** (prayed on Thursdays)
  The Baptism of Jesus in the River Jordan
  The Wedding Feast at Cana
  The Proclamation of the Kingdom of God
  The Transfiguration of Jesus
  The Institution of the Eucharist

- **The Sorrowful Mysteries** (prayed on Tuesdays and Fridays)
  The Agony in the Garden
  The Scourging at the Pillar
  The Crowning with Thorns
  The Carrying of the Cross
  The Crucifixion

- **The Glorious Mysteries** (prayed on Wednesdays and Sundays)
  The Resurrection
  The Ascension
  The Coming of the Holy Spirit
  The Assumption of Mary
  The Coronation of Mary

Praying in Communion with Mary

When people are hoping to meet that special someone, it's not unusual for them to ask for help. It helps to have connections. For Catholics, Mary, the mother of Jesus, is a very special connection. Because of her unique relationship with Jesus, we can go to her for help in growing closer to Jesus. We do not pray to Mary, but rather we pray in communion with her, knowing that through her we can come to know her Son, Jesus.

Stations of the Cross

The Stations of the Cross represent events from Jesus' passion, death, and Resurrection. At each station, we pause and use our senses and imaginations to meditate on the scene depicted or described. We can pray in our own words or we can use prayers provided in one of many Stations of the Cross prayer books.

1. Jesus Is Condemned to Death
2. Jesus Takes Up His Cross
3. Jesus Falls the First Time
4. Jesus Meets His Sorrowful Mother
5. Simon of Cyrene Helps Jesus Carry the Cross
6. Veronica Wipes the Face of Jesus
7. Jesus Falls a Second Time
8. Jesus Meets the Women of Jerusalem
9. Jesus Falls the Third Time
10. Jesus Is Stripped of His Garments
11. Jesus Is Nailed to the Cross
12. Jesus Dies on the Cross
13. Jesus Is Taken Down From the Cross
14. Jesus Is Laid in the Tomb

The closing prayer, which is sometimes included as a 15th station, reflects on the resurrection of Jesus.

Reflective Prayer

Also known as meditation, reflective prayer involves your mind and imagination to engage in prayerful conversation with God and to recognize his presence in your daily life. Follow these steps.

- Set aside 10–15 minutes and find a quiet place where you can be comfortable, yet alert. Close your eyes, or focus on a religious picture or a lighted candle. You may wish to play quiet instrumental music in the background.
- Calm yourself by practicing rhythmic breathing for several minutes.
- Prayerfully read a brief passage from the Gospels and imagine yourself as a participant in the story, using your imagination and senses to enter a setting in which you can talk with Jesus and listen to him speak to you. Instead of Scripture, you may choose to reflect on writings from the saints, inspirational literature, prayer books, or sacred objects, such as a crucifix or an icon. Talk to Jesus as you would talk to a friend.
- End your reflection with one or two minutes of contemplation—simply resting quietly in the hands of God.

> **"There is an intense delight in abandoning faulty states of mind and in cultivating helpful ones in meditation."**
> —The Dalai Lama

Lectio Divina

One form of meditation that Catholics have used for centuries is called *lectio divina* (LECT-see-oh dih-VEE-nah), which is Latin for "sacred reading." This is a way of spending time with the word of God using a special form of reading and listening, so that we can hear God "with the ear of our hearts" (St. Benedict, Prologue to the Rule). Like the Rosary, *lectio divina* involves all three forms of prayer: vocal, meditative, and contemplative. This form of prayer follows four steps.

- **Lectio** (reading)—Slowly and prayerfully read aloud a brief Scripture passage, repeating the passage up to three times after a silent pause between each reading. Allow a word or phrase to speak to you in a special way.
- **Meditatio** (meditation)—Silently reflect for a few minutes upon the word or phrase that is speaking to you. In doing so, take the word or phrase to heart and allow it to interact with your own thoughts, hopes, desires, and memories.

- **Oratio** (prayer)—Enter into a silent dialogue with God for a few minutes, speaking as one friend speaks to another and allowing yourself to be touched and changed by God's word.
- **Contemplatio** (contemplation)—Simply rest silently and prayerfully in God's embrace for a few minutes. By letting go of your own words, allow the word of God to speak to your heart in silence.

***Lectio divina* is a reflective reading of Scripture leading to meditation on specific passages.**
(*USCC for Adults*, p. 474)

Contemplation

Often, the words *meditation* and *contemplation* are used interchangeably. Contemplation and meditation are not mutually exclusive. Meditation is often called *contemplative prayer.* Meditation leads to contemplation. However, a clarification is helpful. Meditation involves actively focusing. Contemplation is simply resting quietly in God's presence. In contemplation, we do not attempt to speak to God, but simply marvel at his glorious presence. It can be compared to enjoying a beautiful piece of art or a nature scene. No words are needed.

⊕ Centering Prayer

Centering prayer is contemplative prayer that goes beyond words. The goal of centering prayer is to simply clear away space to allow us to receive God's gift of grace. Rather than actively focusing, centering prayer invites us to be receptive, opening our minds and hearts to God's presence in silence. Following these steps will help.

- Choose a "sacred word" or brief phrase that symbolizes your desire to be receptive to God's grace. For example, "Come, Lord Jesus," "Peace," "Abba," "Grace," "Be open," or any word or phrase that has personal meaning to you. If you are not a "word" person, you may choose a "sacred gaze," turning inward to gaze upon God.
- Find a comfortable position and close your eyes, sitting silently for a few moments.
- Introduce your sacred word to express your desire to be receptive to God's grace. In your mind, repeat this word or phrase occasionally, especially when you become aware of thoughts.

- At some point, set aside your sacred word and just dwell in silence.
- The overall time frame should be a minimum of twenty minutes, and it is recommended to do this form of prayer twice daily: once in the morning and once later in the day.

The effect of centering prayer, like most prayer, is cumulative: we don't engage in it seeking a spiritual "high," but rather a transformation of our minds and hearts and a deeper recognition of God's ongoing presence and action in our lives. The effects are recognized, not so much during the prayer experience, but in the lived experiences that follow. To learn more about centering prayer, read *Open Mind, Open Heart: The Contemplative Dimension of the Gospel* (Thomas Keating, Continuum International Publishing Group, 1986).

So What?

What difference does it make that Catholics have so many forms of prayer? It means that, no matter what our personality type is—introvert or extrovert—we can find ways to enter into a deeper relationship with God through prayer. It means that we can truly pray without ceasing, knowing the prayer is much more than talking to God, but is our awareness of and response to God's presence in our lives.

Scripture

Rejoice always. Pray without ceasing. In all circumstances give thanks, for this is the will of God for you in Christ Jesus. (1 Thessalonians 5:16–18)

Prayer

Holy Spirit, you teach your people to pray through the guidance of the Church. Thank you for showing me so many ways to be in prayerful communion with you and with the Father and with Jesus. Help me to find the way to pray that is best for me right now in my life. Help me to grow in my prayer life, so that I may better recognize God's presence in my life and respond by loving him and by loving my neighbors.

Chapter Eighteen
Access to Restricted Areas: The Lord's Prayer and How Prayer Works

Construction sites are off-limits to the general population. You have to have either a credential or an access code (or know somebody) to gain access to these restricted areas. When it comes to prayer, we sometimes may think that we need a secret access code to draw near to God, who (we think) dwells in a restricted area. In the Lord's Prayer, Jesus teaches us that we have direct access to God because he is "Our Father, who art in heaven." And heaven's only restriction is that we align ourselves with God: that his will be done on earth as it is in heaven.

Richard Dawkins Got It All Wrong

So, who is Richard Dawkins and what did he get "all wrong?" Richard Dawkins is an atheist, the author of *The God Delusion* (Houghton Mifflin, 2007), a book which has sold over 1.5 million copies. In his book, Dawkins attempts to illustrate what he considers to be the folly of belief in God. Dawkins cites a study on prayer to support his case. The study involved three groups of people who were hospitalized because of various illnesses.

- **Group A was prayed for, but they did not know they were being prayed for.**
- **Group B was prayed for and were informed that they were being prayed for.**
- **Group C was not prayed for.**

Copyright © Doug Hall, 1991. Used by Permission.

"Please bless Mommy and Daddy and Bubba Bear, who's had an especially difficult day."

The study revealed that there was no difference in terms of "feeling better," between those who were prayed for and those who weren't, and actually showed that those who were prayed for and knew that they were being prayed for felt worse. Dawkins, who chose not to cite studies that have shown positive results of prayer, concludes that prayer has no effect whatsoever, and that those who pray are wasting their time because there is no God listening to and responding to their prayers.

After reading his book, *The God Delusion*, and focusing on this study, I felt bad for Richard Dawkins. The concept of God and of prayer that he is attacking is so juvenile that believers should not feel at all threatened. He is not attacking the God that we know and believe in. The "study" he cites on the effects of prayer reflects a very childish concept of prayer. The concept of God that Dawkins attacks is that of a divine Santa Claus and prayer is the act of sitting on Santa's lap and asking for things. Let's review what he got wrong.

We do not pray to change God's mind, but to change ourselves.

- **Prayer is not us seeking God's attention, but responding to God's self-revelation.**
- **We do not pray to change God's mind, but to change ourselves.**
- **Prayer is not an attempt to manipulate or change reality.**
- **The most profound effect of prayer is not necessarily on the person being prayed for, but on the person praying.**
- **The effect of prayer cannot be measured by external (physical) factors alone.**
- **Healing cannot be measured solely on the physical level.**
- **Prayer is not about "my will be done" but "thy will be done."**

But Didn't Abraham and Moses Change God's Mind

In Genesis 18:16–33 and Exodus 32:1–14, we find stories that seem to suggest that Abraham and Moses did indeed change God's mind through prayer. In these stories, Abraham and Moses seem to convince God not to punish people because of their sins. It is important to recognize that, in these stories, God deals with his people on human terms, seeking to teach them (and us) to conform to God's will, which is always mercy. In other words, God taught Abraham and Moses to intercede on behalf of others, seeking the mercy that God has always shown. In both cases, human beings find themselves "reminding" God of his promise. Ultimately, this reminding is for our own benefit, lest we forget God's unchanging nature. These stories teach that God is a God of action, intimately involved in our lives. In both stories and throughout Scripture, God is consistently merciful, drawing people to himself in their time of need to come to know the mind of God and to want exactly what God wants for his people.

Most importantly, Dawkins misses the point that prayer is a relationship with God, not a means of manipulating God. We pray because we are in love with God and desire nothing more than to be intimate with God. And so, Richard Dawkins, I will pray for you. Atheism seems so very empty. I pray that you come to recognize how God is pursuing you, inviting you to enter into a relationship in which you will encounter the divine presence in your life. I mean this most sincerely.

At a Loss for Words

I often begin workshops on prayer by asking my participants how many of them have prayed before. Of course, everyone raises their hands. I tell them that, on the one hand, prayer is not rocket science. We've all prayed, and most of us learned how to do so before we could ride a bike or swim. On the other hand, prayer can seem so complicated. At times we just don't know what to say. It's like a marriage. Typically my wife and I have no trouble making conversation. At those times, however, when we are not in sync with one another and there's a tension between us, even small talk becomes difficult.

Our prayer relationship with God is no different. On the one hand, we can and should be able to talk to God very easily. In fact, St. Ignatius of Loyola, the founder of the Society of Jesus (the Jesuits), encouraged his followers to pray to God as one friend talking to another. Prayer should be simple. On the other hand, at times, we don't know how to pray to God. We don't know what words to use. We don't know how to listen or what we are listening for. The Holy Spirit, through the Church, offers us guidance when it comes to prayer. Although prayer is not rocket science, the notion of communicating with the Creator of the universe is a bit intimidating and just might leave us at a loss for words.

The Holy Spirit, through the Church, offers us guidance when it comes to prayer.

Lord, Teach Us to Pray

Jesus' disciples knew this experience of being at a loss for words when it came to prayer. So they approached Jesus and asked him if he could teach them how to pray. (Luke 11:1) Jesus, of course, responded by teaching them to pray the Our Father, which we call the Lord's Prayer. In this short prayer (only 55 words), Jesus provides us with the vocabulary to talk to God.

Jesus gave us not only the gift of the Lord's Prayer, but also the context in which it should be understood and prayed.
(*USCC for Adults*, pg 483)

Our Father, who art in heaven,
Hallowed be thy Name.
Thy kingdom come.
Thy will be done,
on earth as it is in heaven.
Give us this day our daily bread.
And forgive us our trespasses,
As we forgive those who trespass against us.
And lead us not into temptation,
But deliver us from evil.

Let's take a closer look at just what it is that we are saying in this prayer.

- **Our Father**—Not "my," but "our" Father. The first word of this prayer teaches us that if we have the same father, we must be brothers and sisters. To call God "Father" is to establish familiarity and intimacy. We are not calling upon a god who is impersonal, but upon the One whose offspring we are.
- **Who art in heaven**—These words are not about *where* God is, but refer to God's glorious presence—for heaven is nothing other than being fully in the presence of God. These words, then, are words of praise.
- **Hallowed be thy name**—This is the first of seven petitions which make up the remainder of the Lord's Prayer. *Hallowed* is another word for *holy*. Our petition is that God's name—everything that God is and represents—will be honored and kept holy by all people. These words are both a statement of fact—God's name is holy—and a petition that we keep God's name holy. As God's children and as people who bear the name Christian, we are praying that God's holiness will be made manifest to the world through our faithfulness to Jesus.
- **Thy kingdom come**—In 1776, the soon-to-be United States of America declared independence from King George III of Great Britain. In the Lord's Prayer, we declare our *dependence* on another king—God. A kingdom is defined by boundaries within which a king reigns. All who live within these boundaries recognize the king's will as supreme. God's kingdom has no geographical boundaries. It is located in the hearts and minds of human beings. We pray that God, who is selfless love, will reign over all people. The Our Father is our "Declaration of Dependence."

Is God Male?

God transcends gender. God is neither male nor female. We call upon God as *Father*, however, because this is the name revealed to us by our Lord, Jesus. This does not prohibit us from likening God to a mother, for certainly, that metaphor provides rich imagery for our personal spirituality and prayer. When we pray as Church, we pray in the words that Jesus gave us.

- **Thy will be done on earth as it is in heaven**—This is the main part that Richard Dawkins doesn't get. Prayer is not about achieving our own will, but is about aligning ourselves with God's will. Throughout biblical history, people struggled to accept God's will. Those who did align themselves with God's will found new life. Jesus is the supreme example of what it means to live according to God's will. In heaven—in the presence of God—God's will is done faithfully. We pray that we might do the same.
- **Give us this day our daily bread**—We're not asking for a lot here . . . just for what we need to survive. Bread is the staple of life. We pray that we—all people—will have the basic necessities of life. These words remind us that all of the world's resources come from God and that we are to share them equally.
- **And forgive us our trespasses as we forgive those who trespass against us**—This petition comes with a condition—a disclaimer, so to speak. Interestingly enough, it is a condition we place on ourselves. We ask for God's forgiveness, but only if we forgive others in the same manner that we ourselves have already been forgiven by Jesus. In this petition, we recognize that God's mercy cannot penetrate our hearts if they are hardened with grudges.
- **And lead us not into temptation**—At first glance it might appear that the last two lines of the Lord's Prayer are two ways of asking for the same thing. They are, however, very different. The words of this phrase ("and lead us not into temptation") can be compared to "preventive medicine," while the words of the final phrase ("and deliver us from evil") can be thought of as "curative medicine." Asking God to "lead us not into temptation" is asking him for the guidance we need to stay out of trouble.
- **But deliver us from evil**—As mentioned above, these words can be compared to "curative medicine," meaning that we are asking God to rescue us from evils that are already wreaking havoc in our lives. Bottom line: we need to be saved or delivered, and only God's grace can do that.

For thine is the Kingdom—We can find two versions of the Lord's Prayer in the Gospels: the longer one in Matthew 6:9–13 and the shorter one in Luke 11:2–4. The version of the Our Father that most Christians are accustomed to is based on Matthew. Protestants, however, include the words "For thine is the kingdom, and the power, and the glory, forever and ever." These words, called the doxology, are not found in Luke's version nor in the earliest versions of Matthew's Gospel, and most Scripture scholars agree that these words are not part of Jesus' prayer. However, later versions of Matthew's Gospel included the doxology and it is included in the King James version of the Bible, which is the most common version used by Protestants. This explains why Protestants include the doxology when they recite the Lord's Prayer. At Mass, Catholics pray the words of the doxology separate from the Our Father, only after the priest has offered the prayer, "Deliver us, Lord, from every evil, . . ."

Prayer is not about achieving our own will, but is about aligning ourselves with God's will.

So What?

So, what difference does it make that Catholics pray the Lord's Prayer? It means that we can pray to the One with whom we have an intimate relationship—God our Father. It means that we pray in the very words the Jesus himself gave us. It means that we pray with confidence, knowing that our prayers are heard, and that in praying these words, we can more closely align ourselves with God, in whose image we are made and whose presence we seek.

Did God Want His Son, Jesus, to Die?

Was it the Father's will that his own Son, Jesus, die? What father would will that for his most beloved child? God's will was that Jesus love others to the very end, even in the face of death. Human beings—the Romans and certain Jewish authorities of Jesus' time—willed that Jesus die. The Father's will was for Jesus to remain faithful to his calling to be the incarnation of selfless love. Jesus did this and, in remaining faithful, was raised to new life in the Resurrection.

A deacon was driving to the downtown Cathedral to assist at a very important Mass. He parked his car in a no-parking zone because he was short of time and couldn't find a space with a meter. Then he put a note under the windshield wiper that read: "I have circled the block ten times. If I don't park here, I'll miss Mass. Forgive us our trespasses."

When he returned, he found a citation from a police officer along with this note: "I've circled this block for ten years. If I don't give you a ticket, I'll lose my job. Lead us not into temptation."

Scripture

"Ask and it will be given to you; seek and you will find; knock and the door will be opened to you. For everyone who asks, receives; and the one who seeks, finds; and to the one who knocks, the door will be opened." (MATTHEW 7:7–8)

Prayer

Lord, Jesus, thank you for teaching me to pray. Holy Spirit, guide me and help me to pray without ceasing. Our Father, who art in heaven, . . .

Conclusion

One More Word to Learn

I'd like you to learn one more word—*evangelization.*

Catholics are still getting used to this word. We used to think that this was a "Protestant" word. However, evangelization is a very Catholic concept. Pope Paul VI said very clearly that "The Church exists in order to evangelize" (*On Evangelization in the Modern World*). This means, very simply, we are to make disciples. How do we do this? We begin by striving to become better disciples ourselves. Then, through our words and actions, we invite others to consider following Jesus.

The subtitle of this book is *A Catholic's Guide to Knowing and Sharing Your Faith.* Catechesis is the *knowing* and evangelization is the *sharing* of our faith. My prayer for you and for all of us Catholics is that we will strive to develop a well-built faith, so that we may confidently and enthusiastically share it with others and participate in Jesus' mission of making disciples of all nations!

> May the world of our time, which is searching, sometimes with anguish, sometimes with hope, be enabled to receive the Good News not from evangelizers who are dejected, discouraged, impatient, or anxious, but from ministers of the Gospel whose lives glow with fervor, who have first received the joy of Christ, and who are willing to risk their lives so that the Kingdom may be proclaimed and the Church established in the midst of the world. (Pope Paul VI, *On Evangelization in the Modern World,* 80)

Loyola Press Books by Joe Paprocki

The Catechist's Toolbox
How to Thrive as a Religious Education Teacher
ISBN-13: 978-0-8294-2451-1
ISBN-10: 0-8294-2451-2
7" x 9" Paperback
152 Pages
$9.95

Each year, roughly one-third of the more than five hundred thousand volunteer catechists in Catholic parishes are new to the job; they come with little formal training for their work and are essentially students themselves, quickly needing to learn how to prepare a lesson, lead a discussion, supervise children, apply discipline, and help kids grow in their faith.

The Catechist's Toolbox is an invaluable collection of techniques, tips, methodologies, and advice for all inexperienced catechists who must learn on the job. Master teacher Joe Paprocki shares the wisdom he has gleaned in two decades as a catechist, high school teacher, and religious educator. Employing the metaphor of a homeowner's toolbox, Paprocki explains how a new catechist is like a do-it-yourself builder who needs the right collection of tools to do the job; throughout the book, Paprocki explains what the tools are, what they can do, and how to use them skillfully and effectively.

The Catechist's Toolbox provides first-time catechists with invaluable on-the-job training that will help them feel at home in their new role and will ultimately allow them to thrive as a religion teacher.

The Catechist's Toolbox: A Leader's Guide

How to Thrive as a Religious Education Teacher

ISBN-13: 978-0-8294-2724-0
ISBN-10: 0-8294-2724-0

7" x 9" Paperback

34 Pages

$2.95

Based on the seventeen chapters of *The Catechist's Toolbox: A Leader's Guide* provides seventeen mini in-services (each designed for thirty to forty-five minutes) and equips catechists with skills, tips, and practical advice they can use today.

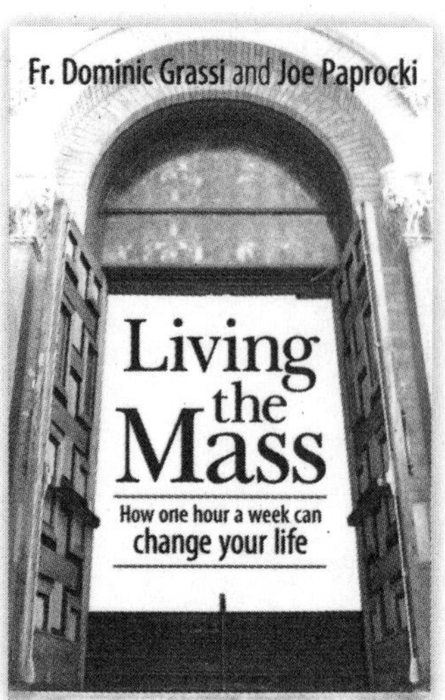

Living the Mass
How One Hour a Week
Can Change Your Life
ISBN-13: 978-0-8294-2076-0
ISBN-10: 0-8294-2076-2
5" x 7" Paperback
208 Pages
$13.95

"We are meant to live the Mass, not merely attend it," write Fr. Dominic Grassi and Joe Paprocki, a priest and a layman who fervently believe that the central worship event of the Catholic faith is meant to transform our world. They begin their book by quoting the words that the priest says at the end of every Mass "Go in peace to love and serve the Lord." This outward-looking, service-oriented focus is the purpose of the Mass. It is intended to equip Catholics with the grace, knowledge, and energy to heal a broken world.

In their lively, readable explanation of the Mass, the authors are particularly alert to the way the Mass strengthens and renews the baptismal commitment of those who attend. Catholics are not strangers to each other but are a body of brothers and sisters, redeemed by Christ, and charged with carrying out his continuing work in the world. The Eucharist is food for a journey of service to family, community, and the world.

God's Library
A Catholic Introduction to the World's Greatest Book
ISBN-13: 978-0-8294-2069-2
ISBN-10: 0-8294-2069-X
5 1/4" x 8" Paperback
160 Pages
$13.95

In *God's Library,* Joe Paprocki, a veteran catechist and Bible authority, guides readers into a basic understanding of "God's Library"—the collection of seventy-three books that Catholics regard as the definitive written revelation of God.

In easy-to-understand language, he explains the organization of the Bible, the different genres of biblical writing, key figures in biblical history, and the methods Catholics have developed to interpret the Bible properly. He shows beginning readers how to use commentaries, concordances, footnotes and cross-references, and other valuable tools of Bible study.

God's Library will delight all Catholics who are beginning their journey to read God's Word.